THE WEAK AGAINST THE STRONG

Simple Folk in the Grip of Turbulent Times

THE WEAK
AGAINST
THE STRONG

Simple Folk in the Grip of Turbulent Times

by

JUDAH PILCH

BLOCH PUBLISHING COMPANY
New York
1973

Acknowledgement

*Our sincere thanks to the Forward Association
for the use of the photographs from
their volume, The Vanishing World,
New York, 1947.*

Foreword to Hebrew Edition

I left my birthplace Vakhnovka, in the Ukraine fifty years ago but my defenseless townspeople who were subjected to pogroms of unusual cruelty, with thirty-six of them being massacred and buried in a common grave, still live indelibly and vividly in my memory. I recall the panic which seized the Jews in the region overrun by the Petlura bands. I remember with horror the summer of 1919, when hundreds of Jewish communities were attacked in a paroxysm of plunder, rapine and slaughter.

I have to evoke in these pages episodes in the lives of ordinary men and women who displayed wondrous staying power and heroism in their struggle against the attackers, and in their readiness to sacrifice their lives for the survival and honor of the people.

In writing these reminiscences I experienced again the bitter terror of those days, and my heart was constricted with pain. Yet a feeling of ethnic pride suffuses me when I commune with the memory of the martyrs whose indomitable spirit in the last moments of their lives insured that the Honor of Israel shall not be cast down to the ground.

New York City, the Tenth of Tammuz, 5729

Preface to English Edition

This little book was written in Hebrew on the 50th anniversary of the pogroms in my native home town. At the urging of colleagues, students and reviewers of the Hebrew volume, I agreed to have it translated into English. Dr. David Kuselewitz, a dear friend and poet prepared a first draft of the translation in 1972, and I have tried to prepare the text for publication. My sincere thanks to Dr. Kuselewitz for his painstaking efforts and cooperation. I am also grateful to Mrs. Judith Golub for her help in editing three of the sketches.

Los Angeles, September 1973

Table of Contents

Jacob the Cantor

All the people of the town loved and respected him, even his two "competitors" from the smaller synagogues. There was not a person who would not greet him with a smile and wish him well: No wonder, for Reb Jacob was a man of kindly disposition, a lover of peace, deeply concerned about everyone's welfare, and above all a highly talented singer, the beloved favorite of one and all. When on the Yamin Noraim (High Holidays), Reb Jacob would pour out his heart in prayer before his Creator in the famous cantorial supplication "Hineni Heani MiMaas" ("Behold, here I stand - a man poor in virtuous deeds"), a shudder would grip the congregation. The people knew that their cantor was searching his conscience and trying with his tears to wash out every stain and blemish of his spirit. His face was covered with his "taliss" (prayer shawl), its heavy silver "attara" (damask collar) hanging down to his chest. His voice, at first meek and mellow gradually rose to a crescendo of power and confidence, as it seemed to be carving a path to the Throne of Glory, there to lay before it the entreaties of his flock. Then he would lower his voice once more in meek supplication to appease the wrath of the Divine Presence. Finally, he would stand erect before the lectern, fold back the "taliss" on his shoulders, take a deep breath and while the whole congregation waited anxiously, he would proclaim like a victorious commander in battle: "Blessed art Thou, who hearest prayers". Everyone would breathe easy after this "crisis" had passed, for all felt instinctively that the cantor's heart-rending sighs and pleas had been accepted by the Almighty.

At that moment I would stand by my grandfather's side and the cantor's singing and my grandfather's sighing made my heart overflow. The letters of the "Mahzor" (Festival prayer book) danced before my eyes, and turning to look at Reb Jacob I was convinced that he was a priest or prophet of old, and I had a strong desire to kiss the fringes of his "taliss" or the hem of the ample sleeves of his "kittel" (white surplice).

Not only on "Yom Kippur" (Day of Atonement), but on all Sabbaths and festivals, whether in a rendition of "Mayest Thou be crowned in glory in the midst of Thy Holy People" or in the melancholy chant of beseeching his Maker to grant him and his congregation "health of body and light from above", those of us who would stand close to him would feel as if the very "Shehina" (Divine Presence) had descended into our humble sanctuary. For hours after the service we would still echo his singing and repeat again and again some musical phrase which he had emphasized.

It was because of Reb Jacob, that the "Tzaddik" (Hassidic Rabbi) Reb Dovid'l of Skvira would honor our town with frequent visits beyond the call of his customary itinerary. Reb Dovid'l loved our cantor's singing and when the latter would intone some favorite Hassidic chant, the "Tzaddik" would lower his head on his elbows, close his eyes and accompany the cantor with expletives and groans, while the Hassidic assemblage surrounding them would not even dare to sneeze or cough. But when Reb Jacob felt like singing a popular tune which lent itself to group singing and accompaniment, all present joined him with gusto and embellished the rising volume of sound with hand-clapping, table-pounding, and plate-banging with knives and forks. One man would twist his lips to produce the precise tone of the melody, while another would tap out the rhythm with his fingers on the back of a tin plate. And when Reb Jacob indulged his musical fancy in a kind of falsetto-pianissimo version of "Redeem Thy People from Exile" the "Tzaddik" Reb Dovid'l would swoon down on the table in a near faint from the emotion which the singing aroused in him. People would shed tears, the room was enveloped in sadness, melodies were heaped upon melodies punctuated by sighs, and all present yearned to go forth into the expanse of the Universe, to roam the world in search of the true and complete "Tikkum" (spiritual perfection), because the travail of the world had become unbearable.

By nature Reb Jacob was a kindly, peaceful and relaxed individual, who on occasion loved to indulge in hilarity and lively conversation. He was wont to spice his discourse with epigrams, "gimatriot"*, quotations from Talmudic literature, and — to differentiate the sacred from the profane — even with the proverbs of the Ukrainian peasantry. He was always carefully dressed, never a stain on his kaftan, his white shirt immaculate, his shoes shined and his graying beard combed out and neatly trimmed.

Reb Jacob was happy with his lot in life. He never complained about his wife's poor health or that he was barely able to provide his family with the minimal essentials of food, clothing and shelter. His meek and modest wife was the proverbial "woman of valor". In the wintertime she was busy with needle and thread, sewing and patching garments, weaving, knitting and embroidering. In the summertime she would whitewash and paint the house inside out. Her children were always well washed and scrubbed and neatly dressed; the whole household presented a picture of clean and comely poverty. Reb Jacob's three daughters and only son were also talented singers and assisted their father in rendering "zemirot"*. Often people gathered at the windows of their house to listen.

The cantor loved Hebrew literature, religious-classical as well as the literary products of the Haskalah (Enlightenment), and especially modern Hebrew poetry. When his deep bass voice joined one of his daughter's lyric soprano in rendition of a modern romantic Hebrew ballad, his wife, who should have been used to it by now, could hardly contain her tears which she wiped demurely with the hem of her apron. At weddings and other family feasts of the wealthy people in town Reb Jacob ate very little and limited his drinking to a mere sip of the sacramental wine. When the "badchan" (professional entertainer at weddings) went into his "act", he would politely offer his blessings to the young couple and his apologies to the assemblage, and leave. My grandfather used to excuse his strange behavior of the otherwise sociable cantor on the grounds that he did not wish to be suspected of flattering the affluent. Called to a wedding at the house of a poor man, a humble artisan or an unskilled laborer, Reb Jacob ate and drank and entertained the bride and groom and their guests as only he could.

Suddenly our horizon was darkened by the black clouds of war, revolution and pogroms. Jews in the war zones have had to bear

*The definition of most Hebrew Terms marked with an asterisk may be found in the glossary.

the brunt of advancing and retreating Russian armies. The devastation wrought by the fighting armies worked havoc with the Jewish population. Hordes of refugees cluttered the roads; multitudes suffered from hunger, lack of shelter and the Poles' and Ukrainians' hostile attitude to the Jews. The revolutions of 1917, after the fall of the Tzar and the ensued civil war caught the Jewish communities between the hammer and the anvil. Pogroms became the order of the day. During this tragic period Reb Jacob changed: his face became lined with deep creases, his figure lost its previously erect stature, and he seemed steeped in melancholy. His bright and cheerful smile vanished, his failing eyesight required him to wear glasses, and his fulsome beard developed bald spots. Many a Sabbath he refused to lead the congregation in the services. He isolated himself from the crowd of worshippers in the back of the hall, wrapped in his "Taliss" as though he wished to express his contrition at the Lord's refusal to heed his prayers. And then came the bloody day when the pogromists made a shambles of Reb Jacob's house. They tore his books and musical scores to bits, and beat up his only son. His daughter pursued by a would-be attacker, jumped out of a window and was severly injured. Reb Jacob walked out like a ghost, stunned and confused. The "Sheloshim" (literally "thirty", i.e. end of the secondary period of mourning after a death in a family; the primary period, the "shiveah", literally "seven", days of mourning beginning with burial) occured on Tisha B'Av (Nineth day of the month of Av, a fast day commemorating the destruction of the Temple in Jerusalem). Reb Jacob took his customary seat on a low bench facing the pulpit and the ark and began to chant the Lamentations. At first he tried to suppress his tears, which choked him so that he was forced to interrupt his keening recitation in the middle of every other verse. But each time he pulled himself together and went on with the biblical requiem. But when he reached the phrase, "I am the man who has seen afflication" (Lamentations 3:1), he burst out in a spasm of loud wailing that reverberated from the walls of the synagogue. The small congregation, a mere three or four "minyanim"* joined the chorus of wailing. Several times Reb Jacob tried to resume his recitation but could not continue, so that "Little Moshe", the assistant cantor, sat down next to him, whispered something in his ear, picked up the Book of Lamentations and the dripping solitary candle, and continued to chant the service.

That very night Reb Jacob appeared in town armed with a gun, as a newly recruited member of the Self-Defense Guard consisting of only three men. Those who saw him said that he was like a new man: his walk was firm, his stature erect, the rifle pressed to his shoulder like the Torah Scroll when he removed it and returned it to the holy ark. He also seemed to be humming a gay tune while his half-closed tear-reddened eyes searched the heavens. The other guardsmen, baffled by this sudden change of personality, feared that he had lost his mind. At midnight, he appeared to be weary of his marching vigil and sat down to rest. All of a sudden he threw away the rifle like a foul or useless object, gripped his hair as if he were about to tear it out by the roots and began to chant the "Tikkum Hatzot" (a solitary service of commemoration and mourning for the destruction of the Temple and the Exile of Jewry, performed at midnight). The echoing minor cadences of Reb Jacob's voice reverberated in the stillness of the night and enveloped the whole town in an atmosphere of deep dejection.

From that day a big change took place in the life of the cantor. He and his family were frequently hungry. He neglected his cantorial duties and spent most of his time assembling the children of the town and teaching them excerpts from the prophetic books of the Bible, along with his own special interpretations which laid the main emphasis on the horrors of the long Exile and so far unrealized hope of redemption. He told them about the recently deceased father and founder of the Zionist Movement, Dr. Theodor Herzl, and about the settlers in the Land of Israel who valiantly defended the isolated colonies which were bravely struggling to survive in a sea of hostile neighbors. Oftentime he would declaim a rousing poem of the famous Hebrew poet Bialik* which had appeared in the magazine "Ha Shiloah".* At those times he seemed resuscitated and rejuvenated, full of hope for happier days.

But then the massacres broke out a second time, when hordes of Machno (Ukrainian "hetman" or Attaman, cossack chieftain), drunk with their recent victories over the units of the Red Army purged our town with fire and sword. The community disintegrated and one by one the residents, the young people in particular, ran off — some toward Moscow, some toward the Rumanian border and beyond. Reb Jacob was among the few who remained. He was in poor health and had lost the sight of one eye. When I came to take leave of him before departing my town forever, he ambled over to his desk, picked up his tuning fork, and after gently striking it against the table and lifting it to his ear began to sing the poet Tschernichovsky's "Nitshu Tzelalim" (Shadows descending). And when he reached the phrase "when our sun is yet to rise", he pressed me with all his might to his chest in a bearhug, so that I thought my heart would soon burst.

He met his bitter end, when with vigorous and firm step this blind sage marched toward his death humming "our sun is yet to rise."

Isaac Kanevsky

Among the rich and erudite community leaders in our town Isaac Kanevsky was the only one who had risen to the top by his own efforts and by many years of hard work for the common good. For a long time he was known simply as "Isaac"; but when the people came to recognize his extraordinary character, his love of humanity and his integrity as a devoted public servant, they added to his name the honorific title of "Reb".

Until he reached middle age Isaac Kanevsky had two occupations: shoe-repairing and gardening. Yet he was known as Isaac the Gardener because he loved this work best. With the early signs of spring he would leave town to tend the gardens and orchards which he rented from the local gentry and the rich peasants and with the first snow of winter he would return. Shoe-repairing was something to fall back on when the other occupation did not provide a full livelihood.

Gardening had been Isaac's first love since childhood. Though apprenticed to Sender the shoemaker, he would disappear during the summer for weeks on end to work in the fields and orchards of the countryside. He returned in the early autumn to Sender's workshop loaded down with all kinds of fruits and vegetables, as a compensatory gift to his master for his absence.

Isaac was orphaned of his father, and his widowed mother made a living by baking cakes and selling them to the peasants in the marketplace. Sender treated him kindly, as he did all his apprentices; but he favored Isaac above the others because of his initiative and vivacity. It was even rumored on more than one occasion that Sender actually accompanied Isaac on his forays into the country. Sender would not prevent his pupil from mastering the trade of gardening in addition to his training to become a good shoemaker.

Many years passed, and at the age of twenty-one Isaac was granted his "Blue Certificate", which exempted him from military service as an only son. He married, and with the 200 rubles of the dowry he bought shoe-repairing tools and acquired a few acres of fruit orchard. Thus Isaac became a "man of property", begot a son and three daughters, was elected second vice-president in the synagogue of the artisans, and ultimately became a community leader. He wore a long kaftan in the style of the Hasidim of Skvira, let his ruddy beard grow untrimmed, and his curly earlocks hang down to his cheeks. By the end of each summer his house was filled with apples, pears, cherries, plums, melons of all kinds, and what we called "Yom Kippur apricots". In the early winter months what was left of the fruit after their sale and a generous distribution of "tithes" to the poor people in the town was preserved in stout little wooden barrels, which were opened as the need arose all winter for consumption by his growing family. Some of the fruit was also cooked into delicious jams and marmalades, a special favorite of old people and children, and long reputed to be a therapeutic remedy for colds, chills and other ailments of the winter season. Isaac even provided the poor with quantities of sugar for making the preserves. Some of the preserves were given to the teacher of the heder in lieu of tuition fees; to Reb Jacob the cantor of the Great Synagogue, in appreciation of his singing, to the ritual slaughterer, to Hannah-Riva, the pot peddler, in recognition of her devoted efforts on behalf of the very poor and sick; and to our family — a family of social position and some wealth — in gratitude for entrusting him with the keeping of the collection box of the Jewish National Fund, from one Yom Kippur to the next.

I was eight years old when I first met Isaac, who by then had acquired a third vocation as a coachman. It was his custom to visit us on Saturday nights for a lively conversation over a steaming glass of tea. My grandfather would be humming the tunes of "Once there was a Hasid", or "Do not fear my servant Jacob"; my younger brother and I would still be reciting "May He grant you" (the patriarch Isaac's blessing to his son Jacob included in the prayers recited at the departure of the Sabbath); while Isaac Kanevsky would be exchanging town news and gossip with my grandmother. When we joined the conversation it invariably turned to the subject of the settlement of Palestine. He would inform us of his conversations with the Shohet (ritual slaughterer) whose son and daughter were living and working on the land in Palestine, and about his wife Rivka, who was willing to undertake the burden of supporting the family while he went to Palestine and labored hard until such time as he could afford to bring the family there. That is how I learned of his detailed plan to save up ruble by ruble for the fare, to acquire a coach and horses for his eldest son, to train him in the work which would be his support now and his occupation when he would ultimately join his father in the Land of Israel. Furthermore, and this he confided to us as his close friends, the town needed an extra coachman for emergencies: to transport a critically ill person to the hospital in Vinitsa, the city which was twenty miles from our town; to bring wood from the forest for heating the homes of the poor; to bring the "feldsher" (para-medical healer) to the home of a bed-ridden patient; and when the need arises, to hustle the midwife to the bedside of a women in labor in the middle of a cold winter night. . . Of course, there was little prospect of making much money from such errands of mercy. But his two other skills provided him with a decent livelihood, and this work was only a sideline. Besides, his son was actually the full-time coachman, while he did those special jobs which benefited the community and brought him a little extra income.

How Isaac originated this ambitious plan to settle in Palestine I never knew. He surely did not derive it from reading Pinsker's "Auto-Emancipation",* nor did he ever see copies of the Zionist periodicals "HaShiloah",* "HaTzephira",* or "Hed HaZman".* He was, nevertheless, a devoted Zionist, and when my father returned from the sixth world Zionist Congress, to which he was elected as a delegate from our district, or when the Shohet received letters from his children in Palestine, he hastened to pay a visit in order to learn everything that had happened. He frequented all Zionist meetings in town and paid close attention to the speeches and discussions. I recall one meeting which was devoted to the controversy over which of our two languages was to be preferred, Hebrew or Yiddish. The representative of the "Bund"* argued that Hebrew was a dead language, whereas Yiddish was alive and used by the masses of our people; an invaluable means of communication and a treasured medium of cultural creativity. This statement created a storm of resentment and disagreement in the hall of the Great Synagogue. Isaac suddenly emerged from the crowd, shouting: "I will soon show you!" He made his way to the Holy Ark, opened it and removed a scroll of the Torah and raising it high, shouted: "Is the Torah written in Hebrew or in your jargon, Yiddish? Is the Torah dead or alive among us? And the Siddur, is it written in Hebrew or Yiddish? And the young generation in Palestine — do they speak Hebrew or Yiddish? And the language of instruction in the "progressive" Heder in our town, is it Yiddish or Hebrew?" Some men ascended the Bimah (pulpit) to lend their support to Isaac in holding the scroll high in the air. And while the crowd looked on in dismay and utter silence at this dramatic demonstration, Reb Jacob the Cantor proclaimed in excited trepidation: "Show respect for the Torah!" and the congregation responded with awe: "It is a Tree of Life for those who support it!" Someone enveloped Reb Jacob with a huge woolen prayer shawl, and the demonstrators with Isaac at their head reverently returned the scroll to the Ark. Meanwhile the Bundists made a hasty retreat from the hall, while the rest of the crowd burst into repeated rounds of song and dance.

Yet where did Isaac acquire the inspiration to settle in Palestine? In the course of time I realized that this simple shoemaker-gardener-coachman was a man of inordinate sensitivity and compassion for the pain and poverty of his fellow human beings. I knew that he earned his daily bread by back-breaking labor day and nights and yet he found the time to make rounds of mercy among the rich and poor alike, to bring healing and consolation to all who suffered material and spiritual want, and that he looked upon the Zionist enterprise as the salvation of our people.

Two years before the outbreak of the First World War Isaac took leave of his family and community and made his way to the port of Odessa. There he divested himself of the outer appearance of a Hasid and sailed for Palestine. Later it became my task to read his letters to his wife Rivka, a kindly, humble but illiterate woman. I recall their contents: fulsome praise for the beauty of the landscape and rationalizations of the exploitation of the

Jewish hired hands in the fields of the Jewish estate owners, coupled with the pious hope that before long things would improve. He painted a glowing picture of the glorious future of the country, described his meaningful life and his progress in the mastery of the Hebrew language. Rivka was very proud of her husband in "Petah Tivka" (she mispronounced the name of the famous colony Petah Tikvah*), and constantly prayed for the day when she and the whole family would be reunited with her husband in the Holy Land.

In her replies — her words in my handwriting — she never complained of her lot as a "grass widow"; nor did she ever tell him of her troubles in making a living for the family. But she never failed to praise the son for his dilligence and hard work, and the daughters for their skill and efficiency in household chores.

Then the War broke out, and there were no letters from Isaac for over a year. The son was taken into the army, prices rose while income fell, and Rivka was lost without Isaac's help and advice. One fine summer day, during the second year of War — it sounds unbelievable — Isaac suddenly appeared, as if from nowhere! To all questions as to how he managed to return, he had only one answer: "I am here — that's all that matters!" His knowledge of geography being very scanty, to put it mildly, his having crossed lands and seas to make his way from Palestine to the Ukraine helped him very little in tracing his complicated itinerary. As an enemy alien he had been arrested by the Turkish police in Palestine, transported to Istanbul, where he managed to escape and join the crew of a freighter bound for Piraeus in Greece. From here he went north into the Balkans and Rumania, where he was taken prisoner by the Russian forces on the frontier and repatriated to the Ukraine.

From the first day of his return Isaac began to devote much of his time to public affairs. Rivka continued to manage their business, and except for occasional help to his wife in making a living, Isaac dedicated himself to the current needs of the community.

At that time the Jewish communities harbored many "hares" — the name given to Jewish young men who on their way to the front for combat duty, or on furlough, decided to desert. When one of these was caught he was court-martialed. When the police decided to stage a raid for "hares" there was great consternation in town. Isaac used to do his own raiding and "kidnapping"; but he kidnapped from the kidnappers. Once he got the guards at the military stockade so drunk that he was able to steal their keys, and release all the prisoners. Another time he and two of his friends galloped behind a marching column of prisoners, attacked it from the rear, and made a quick retreat with several of them. Many a time he returned home from such a daring adventure black and blue with bruises and bleeding from wounds that he had sustained. The punishment that he absorbed goaded him on to ever greater daredevil feats in his desperate attempts to carry out the commandment of "Pidyon Shvuyim" (liberation or redemption of innocent captives).

In the course of time many refugees from Poland, Galicia, Bessarabia and Transsylvania arrived in our town, and Isaac had his hands full with their needs and problems. He fed, clothed and sheltered them. Some of the sick he housed in his own home, or in the homes of freinds and neighbors, until they got well. He entertained them with tales of his life in Petah Tikvah, and his dreams about the glorious future of the Jewish people in their historic homeland. Once I came across him in the street. Isaac was carrying in his arms a pitifully pale infant swathed in rags. His eyes staring into the distance as if seeking the solution to some mystery, Isaac tried to cheer the infant by singing in his raspy voice a Palestinian popular tune. He walked rapidly, the folds of his greatcoat streaming in the wind, his face transfigured by a paternal glow of affection. I joined him as we crossed the great open plaza in front of the Church and approached the imposing mansion of the town patron Mr. Markov. I was baffled: What was Isaac's business with Markov? In the vestibule of the house we were met by a servant who led us into the parlor. For some reason, when Markov entered the room the child began to wail with sudden fright. Isaac took out a piece of zwieback from his pocket and stuck it into the infant's mouth to stifle his crying. He then unwrapped the child's swaddling clothes and displaying his tiny emaciated body to the astonished and shocked gaze of the rich host, saying: "Look at this pitiful little creature! There are many like him among the refugees, and adults too! There is not a moment to lose if we wish to save lives! We must provide them with warm clothing and food. They are our brothers — mine and yours — I have come to you while there is still time to . . ."

Markov did not allow him to finish, but took several banknotes out of his pocket and handed them over to Isaac. Instead of offering thanks to the benefactor for his generous gift, Isaac thrust the money into the child's little hand, and raising the naked infant with the zwieback still stuck in his little mouth high in the air, lowered him into Markov's protruding arms. He gave me a sign to follow him and abruptly left the house. Soon the whole town knew that Markov had made a handsome contribution for the relief of the refugees, and that his daughter, Liza, was not only collecting clothing for them but actually caring for one of their infants, which was entrusted to her by Isaac Kanevsky.

Then the days of ultimate terror arrived with the news of the pogrom in Proskurov. Isaac disguised himself as a peasant and left town. When he returned a few days later, he looked like a sick old man: his eyes sunk in their sockets, his hair suddenly turned white and his figure bent. Although he said little, we realized that the wave of terror would soon engulf us also. To all our questions he had but one answer: Self defense. The leaders of the community took issue with him; they doubted that our forces and resources would suffice to immunize us and defend us against attack. Isaac did not expect such opposition, and was greatly discouraged. Meanwhile the horror swept over the whole country. Isaac still maintained that our only recourse was the immediate organization of a self-defense force, while the town notables insisted on the tried stratagem of sending out a delegation of friendly gentiles to appease the wrath of the approaching hordes of pogrom-bent Cossacks. Even after we got the news of the heroic stand of the self-defense forces of the towns of Chmelnik, Priluki and others, there was no change in the attitudes of our leaders, no concession to the views of Isaac and his followers.

When the pogrom finally came Isaac dashed around the town dressed in his peasant attire — his hair and beard shaven clean. His coach served him well to save many people from certain death. The wounded he brought to the house of the local priest, who was a friend of the Jews and did a great deal to help them in this peril. An eyewitness later testified that when Isaac saw a Gaidamak (cossack clansman) dragging Reb Ozer's younger daughter, intending to rape her, he ran after him, caught up with him and hit him so hard with his hefty club that the cossack fell down in a dead faint. He hoisted the swooning girl to his shoulder and disappeared with her into one of the alleys bringing her safe and sound to her parents.

After this first pogrom Isaac succeeded in organizing a self-defense force in town. And although he knew next to nothing of military tactics, he assumed command of it. He would anticipate an attack by the young peasants of the villages surrounding our town, and lay an ambush for them in the woods, routing their offensive before it reached its destination. His victorious rescue of the town of Dinivitz and the decisive defeat of the band of the notorious Gaidamak chieftain Anton Kvachuck near the town of Petchera are a matter of record. This feat was accomplished through the good offices of the girl he saved during the first pogrom. The girl was very attractive. Her blond braids and the flowered kerchief she wore gave her the appearance of a Ukrainian city damsel. Isaac knew of the girl's eagerness to join a self-defense group and suggested to her that she go to the headquarters of Kvachuck's staff who occupied the home of the rich Mr. Lifshitz. Upon nearing the place she should tell the guards, if any were to be there, that she has to see their leader on a personal matter. He, Isaac, will follow her, being her "father" to restrain her from giving herself to the division's head. When she will gain entrance, and the officers would most likely rise in bewilderment to welcome the beautiful girl, she should draw her revolver, which Isaac had given her, and shoot to kill. He, Isaac, would enter the house from the attic and the nine members of the self-defense group would lie in waiting, — all equipped with guns, — "And God help us," said Isaac convincingly. The successful realization of this scheme which took the lives of more than 20 bandits is inscribed for posterity in the archives fo the Jewish community.

Fifty years have passed since those days, and I still recall vividly the heroic image of Isaac Kanevsky. I heard nothing of his fate during the Soviet regime. It was reported that he had made an attempt, together with his family, to cross the Dniester river frontier into Rumania, in order to make his way to Palestine. But they were caught by the frontier Soviet guards and imprisoned.

During World War II, I recieved the news of the martyrdom of this eighty-six year old sage, together with all his kin at the hands of the Nazis, in the city of Berditchev.

Now I recall the accusation which Reb Isaac cast heavenward on the day of the pogrom in 1919, when the victims were being lowered into their graves: "How is it possible to recite with integrity and innocence the Kaddish* which reads: "Magnified and sanctified be His Great Name. . .?"

Hannah-Riva the Pot Peddler

Hannah-Rivah, an unshapely, plain looking woman but energetic and virtuous, gained a reputation as a woman of valor. Beside her regular occupation as a peddler of pots, which she inherited from her father two years after her husband, a barrel maker, became ill, Hannah-Rivah also did embroidery and knitting — embroidery in the summer and knitting in the winter. At both she was very skillful and proficient. While waiting for customers at her stand in the marketplace, she would be busy with her wool. When a customer appeared, she looked him up and down, to see if he was bent on making a purchase, or merely "looking" to compare prices and values. When she was satisfied that he was a genuine prospective buyer, she put her knitting in a pot and rose from her seat to take care of him. But if she concluded that the customer was not likely to come to "takhliss" (a practical, positive result), she would stay in her place, continue with her knitting, and engage in lukewarm, inconsequential conversation with him.

This was her routine in the late fall and early winter. But when real frost arrived, with the possibility of freezing toes and fingers, Hannah-Rivah filled two stout pots with glowing coals: One she placed between her legs, under her wide skirts, to warm the lower part of her body; the other she placed close to her hands, with their half-exposed fingers, which notwithstanding the vigorous exercise in knitting were mostly likely to be frost-bitten. Her head was wrapped in a tight woolen kerchief tied under the collar of her sheepskin coat, and her feet were protected by a pair of thick felt boots.

In summer, when the sun permeated her body with a pleasant warmth, there was no need for protective clothing, which slowed down a person's mobility. It was easier, then, to embroider: towels stitched with figures of colorful roosters in pink and red yarn; handkerchiefs and bandanas bordered in blue and purple for the heads of modest maidens and virtuous matrons; and on occasion, sacred objects, such as small bags for "tephillin" (phylacteries), and matzah covers. Hannah-Rivah participated in two regional fairs a week, in addition to the local markets, which required no special effort.

Her late father, Reb Hirsch, may he rest in peace, was a good and honest Jew, God-fearing and loved by all. Before his death he called for his only daughter, Hannah-Rivah, her husband Zelig, the barrel maker, and the gentile Avrillo, his faithful steward. The dying old man took his daughter's hand in his own and in the presence of Zelig and Avrillo declared solemnly that his daughter was destined to gain much respect in the community. In addition to her responsibilities as housewife she was about to take full charge of the pot peddling business. Avrillo, who knew all the "ins" and "outs" of this existing trade, would be her guide and mentor at all times. Then he turned to his son-in-law, Zelig, and warned him to watch his health. Avrillo promised that he would continue to lend his aid and counsel to the woman, as he did to her father. Avrillo was reputed to be completely loyal and devoted to his master, and quite knowledgeable about various Jewish rituals and customs. He also used Yiddish expressions.

After Reb Hirsch's death, Avrillo went to the Rabbi to ask permission to recite the "Kaddish" (mourner's prayer) for his late master, on the grounds that since the deceased had left no sons to perform this sacred duty, he would be willing to do the honors in front of the icon in his living room. Avrillo was a "Jew-loving" gentile, who was never heard to curse the Jews, even when he got drunk. More than once he defended the Jews against the verbal tirades of his friends and more than once suffered a sound beating for his tolerant, neighborly attitude. When he had a justifiable grudge against a Jew he would quote, or rather, misquote the Talmudic proverb: "Mountains never meet, but human beings meet" (and upon meeting are liable to scuff each other . . .). Invoking this quotation would dissipate his feeling of grievance.

Avrillo participated in Reb Hirsch's funeral, walking respectfully and humbly about twenty yards behind the pall bearers. When the cortege reached the cemetery, Avrillo, not daring to enter, remained outside near the fence. When he heard the Cantor's requiem, he removed his cap, crossed himself, and whispered a few words of prayer.

With Avrillo's help Hannah-Rivah became a pot-peddler. Her heart was not in commerce though, but in charitable community affairs. Since her youth she had been accustomed to helping her poor neighbors. Many times she spent all day and night in the house of a poor family cleaning and nursing, washing dishes, cooking meals, feeding the children — whatever was needed. Reb Hirsch fully approved of her charitable acts and helped her with modest sums of money every week to do with as she pleased. People knew that Hannah-Rivah never came to the home of a poor family empty handed. The commandment "Thou shalt surely help him" became second nature to her; even after she married and had plenty of troubles of her own, she did not forsake her work for the needy or stop her gifts of food and clothing. When she realized that the Almighty had deprived her of children, she threw herself into charitable work with greater zeal than ever.

From the town's triumvirate of trusted and dilligent "do gooders", Reb Jacob the Cantor, Reb Moishe Breindl's and Isaac Kanevsky, she learned all aspects of charitable endeavor. How a woman should be accepted into such a worthy and exclusive club of public benefactors was difficult to understand. This is how my grandfather Reb Moishe explained it: The three men came by one morning to the home of a poor, sick widow to bring her some money and food and found Hannah-Rivah there washing clothes, baking bread, and cooking gruel for the children before sending them off the heder.* They saw that she kept an eye on the patient as well, changing the cold compress on her feverish forehead when needed. That morning the four concluded a solemn covenant of mutual trust: Isaac Kanevsky would supply her with the produce of his orchards and gardens; Reb Jacob would allocate a regular subsidy to her from the fund he administered, to do with as she saw fit; and Reb Moishe would accompany her on her rounds of mercy, whenever she needed assistance. Later, when Gittl, who visited homes every Friday to collect Hallas (Sabbath bread) for the poor, fell ill, Hannah-Rivah undertook this chore as well. The town's people maintained that the homely Hannah-Rivah, looked handsome, even elegant, when she performed acts of mercy.

Hannah-Rivah displayed a special affection toward mothers and small children, probably because she was childless and her maternal instincts had been supressed for so many years, but also because of her great compassion for those who are sick and wanting, especially innocent infants and helpless children. She studied midwifery to help save the lives of destitute women in difficult childbirth.

Once, at a fair in Kalinovka, Hannah-Rivah happened to pass a peasant's cart in which she saw a woman lying on a heap of sacks of straw, writhing in the agony of labor. The woman's husband stood by half-frozen in the bitter cold and helpless in the face of a task beyond his knowledge and experience. Hannah-Rivah abandoned her pots and quickly took charge of the situation. She rounded up three peasants and ordered them to carry the woman into one of the houses nearby. At first she sent for the town midwife, but before the messenger left the house, she changed her mind. The frequency and loudness of the woman's scream indicated that she would have to perform the job herself very soon. In the evening, when the mother and her new-born son were sleeping peacefully, Hannah-Rivah reflected on her "job well done" of that day, and decided that henceforth, she would serve as the midwife in her own town. Even though Avrillo had to spend most of the day looking for stolen and lost pots, she did not complain. Feelings of joy filled her heart; as if by miracle she had achieved a great and important goal. From that day Hannah-Rivah was present at the bedside of every Jewish woman in childbirth, at first assisting the professional midwife, and ultimately doing the work herself. This new profession afforded her an unusual measure of satisfaction: Her face shone with happiness every time she held a new-born infant in her arms.

In the second year of World War I Avrillo developed a stomach ailment, which kept him in bed for many weeks and left Hannah-Rivah without a driver to the fairs. Avrillo's son-in-law, an unsettled, pleasure-seeking young man, always in pursuit of vodka and women became the driver. Hannah-Rivah, of course, disapproved of him. She hired another driver in his place, but he proved so inept at packing the merchandise that her losses exceeded her earnings. Consequently, she became the driver herself. When deserters from the army and soldiers on leave began waylaying travelers and robbing them, she decided to stop going to fairs altogether until the emergency subsided.

The necessity of making a living, however, prompted her to accept a job baking hardtack from the local army contractor, on a commission basis. Her efficiency soon impressed the army inspector so much that he appointed her supervisor over all hardtack bakers in the region. This job was a double responsibility: acquiring new and patched sacks for packing this "bread of affliction", and seeing to it that the bakers observed government specifications and did not charge more than what was agreed on in the contracts. She found this an excellent opportunity to employ many of the poor people in the town: From one she ordered new sacks; from another, hundreds of patchwork jobs on old and torn sacks; from a third, baking. Her house became a veritable storeroom of dry army food with men and women coming and going all day, delivering and receiving merchandise. Hannah-Rivah welcomed then all with a smile and complimented them on their efficiency. Avrillo, who had recovered from his illness helped her and was happy with his new work.

Unfortunately, this period of prosperity did not last long. Soon an order from the provision officer was received to discontinue the work. Hannah-Rivah left with a deficit of several hundred rubles, was unable to pay her workers. She solved the problem by extracting half of her debt from the delinquent government agency, and covering the other half with a loan from Mr. Markov, the richest man in the community.

In the summer of 1917 a "miracle" happened: New winds began to blow in the country. The cantor no longer offered the prayer for the welfare of the emperor, because the tzar no longer ruled. The new regime under Kerensky did not discriminate between races and creeds: complete equality and freedom for all citizens was guaranteed by the new constitution. Hannah-Rivah, like everyone else, was overjoyed by the turn of events. At last salvation had come! The poor and downtrodden of the land will be uplifted, and her wretched people will not be exposed to derision and deprivation anymore. One need no longer fear attacks from bandits on the way to the fairs of Zazov, Kalinovka, and Priluki! So Hannah-Rivah resumed her journeys to those towns and carried a thriving business.

The "honeymoon" passed as quickly as it came. Many who shouted slogans of equality and justice quickly changed their tune. "Beat the Jews and the communists and save the Ukraine!" spread throughout the land. Hannah-Rivah, who had not yet sobered up from the heady intoxication of the Revolution, continued her travels as usual. One autumn day past the railway station in Turbov, returning from a fair she encountered a group of rioters attacking six Jewish merchants. The Jews, who had been thoroughly searched for hidden money, stood shivering in the bitter cold, their hands and faces bleeding, begging their tormentors for mercy. Hannah-Rivah, who was dressed as a simple peasant woman, and whose accent in the local Ukrainian dialect was undistinguishable from that of the local peasantry, ordered Avrillo to stop, removed his crucifix, and hung it on her own neck. Slowly she approached the attackers addressing them gently and kindly: "Good people don't offend our Lord and Savior by robbing these poor innocent Jews, who are not communists, but decent men whom I have known for many years. Dear brothers, don't shed innocent blood! You had best go after the wicked, Jewish communists." Suddenly, she pretended to lose her temper and began to shriek: "Go and take the treasure of my wicked employer, for whom I — a poor Christian widow — have been slaving my years away. Come and see how much money is hidden in the pots I am bringing her." Her speech was so convincing that the bandits abandoned their victims and rushed to Hannah-Rivah's wagon. While they were searching the pots for hidden money, the Jewish merchants mounted their own coaches and escaped. When the disappointed bandits realized that their victims had escaped, and that the money found in the wagon totaled much less than expected, they poured out their wrath on poor Hannah-Rivah and her accomplice, Avrillo. Had it not been for Avrillo's loyalty in not disclosing the disguise of his "traitorous" mistress, the bandits would have murdered her on the spot. This incident was reported by Jews returning from the fair. The town notables came to Hannah-Rivah's house to congratulate her on her heroic deed. After the day's ordeal she sat up in bed with difficulty leaning against some pillows and somewhat incoherently, pleaded with them to take preventive action. .

When the civil war erupted in full force, the bands of Petlura (Ukrainian nationalist leader), joined by roving gangs of outlaws, bandits, and cutthroats, spread through Jewish towns to kill and plunder. Hannah-Rivah changed radically: The pleasant, relaxed woman, who always received everyone with a kind smile, became nervous and irritable. Her face looked depressed, inside she was in turmoil. Those who had known her casually were baffled by this change, but those who knew her more intimately were aware of her suffering. She could not make peace with the idea that her people would submit to slaughter like sheep; that a populous community would not lift a finger to defend itself against roving gangs of rural teenagers. She was particularly appalled that as soon as some country bumpkin began waving a gun or pitchfork, scores of Jewish adults would abandon their market stalls and run home for cover, not doing anything to put an end to such provocations. One night shots were heard, and nobody left the safety of home to investigate the shooting; they hid in cellars all night. If she were a man, perhaps they would rally to her cry for mobilization for self-defense; if she were erudite, perhaps she would be able to reinforce her arguements with appropriate scriptural quotations, and perhaps she would be able to convince the community that her plans were as sound as they were honorable.

Once, when I brought some medicine for her sick husband, she remarked to me thoughtfully: "I am troubled by numerous questions for which I have no answers; and when I direct them to my husband, I receive the inevitable answer that such is the will of the Almightly! Alas, I don't know how to find an answer in the Holy Books, but I cannot accept the conclusion that God wills such evil events . . . There must be a different answer somewhere in the Scriptures, otherwise life is hardly worth the trouble . . ." She was straining to hold on to her faith in Providence by finding a convincing reason for the troubles that had befallen our people. Regretfully, I could not find a reason either, and in place of reassurance and encouragement, I could offer her only the sympathetic attentiveness of an adolescent who was disturbed by the same doubts. Hannah-Rivah continued speaking about the uncertainties of reality and the mystery of life. Much of it was beyond my comprehension. But I recall her asking: "Is it possible that Avrillo is right, that our God is more vengeful than merciful and loving; is it possible . . .?"

When she heard that some neighboring communities had organized self-defense units, she was greatly encouraged. With Isaac Kanevsky, Mr. Kunis, and a few other militants, she began campaigning for similar action in our town. While she was still to convince the community that a catastrophe was in the making — a band of partisans under the leadership of the infamous killer Tutiunik was on the way to our wide-open town. Hannah-Rivah decided that it was her duty to take drastic action. Since she was well-known in all the surrounding villages and respected by their leaders, she would try to influence them to defend their Jewish neighbors. She devised a double strategy. She would induce the village elders to prevent their constituents from participating in the empending pogrom, she would find hiding places for the women and children in the homes of peasants. She lost no time implementing her plan. Avrillo drove her to the villages, where the notables whom she contacted assured her that they would warn the young men not to molest the local Jews. Again with the help of Avrillo, she transported all the old men and women and children from her house, where they had gathered, to the homes of peasants who agreed to shelter them. Nevertheless, she was greatly disturbed to see so many young peasants join the riffraff of outlying villages with sacks on their backs, ready to plunder Jewish homes. Suddenly, Avrillo appeared with the sad news that two of her confidants had deserted to the enemy, and the people whom she had entrusted to their protection were now fleeing.

Confusion proliferated. Cries of havoc rose, and the looting began. Hannah-Rivah felt as if her whole world were crumbling. She gathered her neighbors into the cellar and barred the entrance with a double row of her husband's barrels. The valuables, that people had salvaged she divided into two parts: one part she placed in the drawers of the table, and the other she hid in a pot which she placed in the oven. She barely finished when the rioters burst into the house, breaking furniture and dishes in their search for money and valuables. Hannah-Rivah, disguised as a peasant, went upstairs and together with Avrillo joined the looters in their frenzy of destruction. She shouted praises of the "brave deliverers of the Ukrainian people from their Jewish oppressors," and led them toward a china closet where some vodka was hidden. The rioters lost no time getting drunk, and every time the door opened for more rioters, they drove them off shouting that this Jewish house was their exclusive domain. When the mob finally exhausted its greedy wrath and deserted, Hannah-Rivah wept tears of joy, although her house had been demolished. She had succeeded in saving 22 lives and salvaging some of her neighbors silver utensils used on Sabbaths and holidays.

Hannah-Rivah developed a throat ailment during the pogrom. From that day her voice was hoarse and she had difficulty talking.

Two days before my departure from Vakhnovka, Hannah-Rivah came to my grandfather's house and brought me three letters to deliver outside Russia, after I would have succeeded in crossing the frontier to Bessarabia. She herself would have liked to escape from the "Vales of Tears", perhaps to go to Palestine. At the last moment she supplemented our previous talks by remarking: "God has not abandoned us. We ourselves had failed to provide for our future."

Fifty years have passed, and the figure of this heroic woman Hannah-Rivah, remains indelible in my memory. Every year on the anniversary of the pogrom in my town I recall with reverence the indomitable spirit of those who realized the splendor of supreme courage. Hannah-Rviah was one of them.

Haim-Ber the Hide Merchant

He who has not seen Haim-Ber dance on Simhat Torah* Eve has truly never seen the soul dance. His eyes shining, his face flaming, his mouth half open, spouting snatches of song in time with the rythm of the dance, his feet stomping on the floor, first slowly then fast, to the right and to the left, in a circle, back and forth — all with profound inner exaltation. His hands were raised on high waving an imaginary tambourne. The corners of his kaftan and his red kerchief were stuck in the wide belt which encircled his waist. From time to time he would whip out that kerchief and wave it in front of his face as if carrying on a dialogue with it. And when the people saw him stamping and leaping, his face beaming brightly, they would surround him and with arms locked and faces shining join in the crescendo of the singing and dancing as if saying: "Our hearts are overflowing with joy like yours — Dance brother dance!"

After a while the beadle, Reb Yonah, would bring a Torah scroll into the circle and hand it to Haim-Ber. In the presence of the scroll of the law, Haim—Ber's exuberance would become transfigured into awe, his face would shine with tender grace, his feet slowed and his singing would be muted as he softly chanted "Beloved of my soul, Merciful Father, bend Thy servant to Thy will." He appeared altogether like a lover declaring himself to his beloved. Meanwhile the circle around him would widen with new arrivals, and the singing reached a new climax, expressing infinite love for God and man. Haim-Ber whirled around in the middle, hugging the Sefer Torah, shouting, "Thou who art pure and upright, save us . . . answer us when we call!"

On Simhat Torah Eve when the congregation paraded around the pulpit with the Torah scrolls the cantor would call an intermission after the fourth of the seven prescribed rounds in order to give the people a chance to rejoice without the restraint and formality of the prescribed ritual of the Hakafot,* Anxious to overcome his own inhibitions against spontaneous revelry, he would join the dissonant shouts of joy with his own extemporaneous medley of Skvira-Hasidic tunes. Haim-Ber would take them up immediately, and the two would stand face to face, the cantor's improvisations adorned with falsettoes and vibratoes urging Haim-Ber to speed up his dance. His feet flying, his eyes closed with growing ecatasy, his voice dying out in exhaustion, Haim-Ber would concentrate upon the rhythm synchronizing it with the Cantor's singing. The people were quiet, fully absorbed by the duel dialogue of sound and motion of the two soloists. Only the Rabbi's broad hints that it was time to resume the Hakafot would bring them back to reality.

Nor can anyone who has ever seen it forget Haim-Ber's performance on Purim* Eve. With biting, ironic shafts of wit he would scourge all the members of our "establishment": the officers and the trustees of our community organization, the professional pietists "holding on to the heels of heaven," as he phrased it, and the apostates who blaspheme against "The Lord and His anointed." He seldom had a rival for the people's attention as they tried to catch every shade and nuance of his satire and howled with laughter at each well-aimed barb of sarcasm. Even the men who were the targets of this onslaught enjoyed Haim-Ber's performance, for the very fact that Haim-Ber attacked them proved how prominent they were in the community. Only those who were ignored by Haim-Ber were disturbed — worrying about the reason for their demotion. And it was not only the proud and important who were prodded with Haim-Ber's wit. For the artisans and petty merchants, the frequenters of fairs and the drifters he offered a single, collective, rhymed accolade replete with criticism of their way of life, their abject poverty, their ignorance and their coarseness.

All year long Haim-Ber was busy with his trade of dealing in hides. His small shop on the Street of the Butchers was stocked with all kinds of hides, which he sold both wholesale and retail. His customers were cobblers, tanners, owners of stalls in the market and peasants from the nearby villages. In his shop

Haim-Ber was sober and serious; anyone who saw him there would hardly imagine that this earnest man, with the ruddy cheeks, blond beard and curly little earlocks was the same one who had entertained the people on Simhat Torah and Purim. He conducted his business in a slow and deliberate style, occasionally enlivened by a touch of humor and local aphorisms. But let one of the peasants dare to cast a hint of aspersion on the Jewish people and Haim-Ber's temper would flare, warning the man in no uncertain terms to guard his tongue. Since the Gentiles were aware of Haim-Ber's strength, the culprit would hasten to apologize and to emphasize that he had been misunderstood. It was related in town that once Haim-Ber had explained to one of his acquaintances, an elderly peasant of good character, how unscrupulous merchants cheat customers who are inexperienced in monetary transactions. "Here is a ruble note," said Haim-Ber, showing him a banknote, "one ruble on one side and," turning it over, "another ruble on the other side; together, two rubles. In this way one can give five rubles for ten." "Ah", said the Gentile in all innocence, "all the dishonest Jewish merchants must practice this game constantly." Haim-Ber first changed the peasant's mind by knocking him down with a powerful slap in the face and then, having taught him a lesson, immediately raised him up and revived him with a glass of whiskey and a piece of cake.

When he was alone in the shop he sat on a rickety chair behind a wobbly table and read a book. When a customer entered, he quickly hid the book in the table drawer lest it should be seen. It was rumored in town that he was reading forbidden literature in Russian and German. His intimate friends knew though that Haim-Ber was very fond of Modern Hebrew literature: poetry, essays, drama and fiction. He was particularly devoted to the popular periodicals "Ha-Shiloah" and "Ha Olam", and when he would come across some poignant essay or a particularly touching short story, he would show his appreciation by singing one of the Rebbe's tunes of spiritual ecstasy and exaltation. When a Zionist preacher came to town to deliver an inspirational oration on the subject of the "Return to Zion," Haim-Ber displayed his enthusiasm by stamping his feet and embracing the speaker.

His wife, Gittl, was short and stout. Having been brought up in the country, she was an expert in making buttermilk, sweet and sour cream, butter, baked goods and preserves. While working she would whistle out loud and her high-pitched renderings of her husband's tunes were heard far and wide. When the spirit moved them, both husband and wife would sit on a bench behind the house and perform duets — he in his ringing tenor voice, she with her piercing whistle. It was reported that at the wedding of their only son, Jacob-Moshe, during the nuptial feast after the ceremony, Haim-Ber had danced and sung, accompanied by an obbligato of vigorous whistling. No one could tell whether the whistler was his wife Gittl, since the sound came from the adjacent room. It was also known that on Saturday nights Gittl would embroider her chanting of the supplication, "God of Abraham, Isaac and Jacob — the Holy Sabbath is departing" with sad, sharp, heartbreaking whistles. Upon her husband's return from the synagogue she would stop whistling and hasten to welcome him with a "Good Week" greeting and a blushing caress. After the Havdalah* ceremony in honor of the departing Sabbath, he would take her hand and both would sit on the sofa singing and whistling in perfect harmony the traditional hymns of Havdalah night. Not in vain did Reb Jacob the Cantor crown Reb Haim-Ber with the title of "Sweet Singer of Israel".

Jacob-Moshe's wife was also a singer, and once when the younger men in town gathered at a Zionist meeting, this young woman entertained them by singing "The Place where the Cedars Grow", a popular early Zionist ballad, in her lyrical soprano. When this indiscretion was related to Haim-Ber, he roared and stamped his foot. No one could tell whether he was angry, agreeing with the fanatics who held to the Talmudic dictum that "a woman's voice is a temptation", or expressing his pride in his daughter-in-law, who had dared to exhibit her talent to a male audience.

Jacob-Moshe travelled to the fairs to sell his father's goods. He was known to associate with socialists and to spend evenings studying pamphlets and books about the class struggle and the revolution which would free humanity from oppression. He even took an interest in the new ideology of Socialist-Zionism. Haim-Ber and his son had fervent verbal battles over these issues, with the father asserting that any change in the social order required the intervention of Providence as well as human action, while the son maintained that the "massess", once they had been primed by their class-conscious leaders, would throw off their shackles and liberate themselves. Both father and son enjoyed these debates tremendously and left each other flushed with intellectual passion and mutual love and admiration.

There was a story that once at a meeting called by a public speaker, who came from Kiev to sell membership fees to the Zionist Congress and to raise funds for the Jewish National Fund, (the Palestine Land redeeming agency) a local youth, called Leibush the Student, who was a devotee of socialism, had engaged the speaker in a heated debate. Haim-Ber at first just listened to the bitter exchange, his head hidden in his arms as if he were sleeping. Suddenly, he leaped up and ran toward the stage loudly berating the student for showing so much concern for the masses of workers and peasants while ignoring the interests of his own people. Jacob-Moshe barred his father's way, shouting, "It is improper to disturb the speaker!" For a moment father and son faced each other as if they were about to come to blows. Then realizing that his son was right, Haim-Ber returned to his seat. When the student finished, Haim-Ber asked for the floor and clearly and calmly refuted his anti-Zionist view. After the meeting father and son walked home in the dark streets and parted with deep affection.

When war broke out, Jacob-Moshe was drafted and, after six weeks of basic training, was sent off to the front. Haim-Ber walked about in the marketplace and in his store in a trance, neither eating nor sleeping. His ruddy face paled, his posture drooped, and all his natural vigor and enthusiasm were gone. He seemed to have aged suddenly. At the end of the summer the first casualties began to arrive in town and Haim-Ber spent many hours with them listening to reports of the battlefield and tales of the suffering of the Jewish soldiers. Vicious propaganda was being spread about the Jews' responsibility for the defeat of the Russian armies and Jewish guilt in promoting hatred and dissension among nations and causing wars between them.

That year there was no dancing in the synagogue on Simhat Torah. When Haim-Ber returned home from the gloomy service he found there a crippled, limping veteran from a neighboring village with a letter from Jacob-Moshe saying he was in a military hospital somewhere in Poland. Haim-Ber left the next day to go to his son.

Weeks passed, and there was no news from either Haim-Ber or Jacob-Moshe. Their wives, supporting themselves with difficulty, were constantly red-eyed from weeping. The townspeople, who had plenty of troubles of their own, could not understand Haim-Ber's disappearance. The refugees from the communities close to the front could give no clue as to his whereabouts.

Five months later there was still no word of Haim-Ber. His wife Gittl fell ill, and her daughter-in-law took care of her. Since the store had to be closed, there was not a penny in the house. But then in the early spring, along with the new growth in field and forest, the two men suddenly appeared looking lean and bedraggled, their hair overgrown and their clothes in tatters. Soon it was learned that Haim-Ber had been imprisoned, and his son, whose leg was amputated in the hospital, had made the rounds of various offices trying to get his father released from jail. Various reasons were given for Haim-Ber's arrest. Some said that he had broken furniture in the hospital when he was forbidden to enter his son's room; other maintained he was quilty of aggravated assault on the army doctor who took care of his son. His daughter-in-law's version was that he was accused of severely beating two young officers who had pulled his earlocks, called him "dirty Jew" and "Christ killer" and had attemped to lower his pants in order to examine his genitals.

On Sabbath morning, after the father and his son had recited the "Hagomel"* blessing in gratitude for having survived a mortal danger, Haim-Ber delivered a speech to the congregation describing in harrowing detail the constant attacks on the life and property of Jews in the communities near the front. He proposed plans for self-defense, holding up the exploits of the "HaShomer"* in Palestine as an example to emulate and telling of attempts to establish self-defense units in several Ukrainian towns. Yet, although the people listened to his exhortation attentively and a dozen or so volunteered to help him, his plan was not carried out until the first pogrom had taken place.

Meanwhile the revolution broke out and the pogroms were the order of the day. Young men of our town, sensing the tragedy and the danger, left the homes of their fathers to seek adventure and salvation in the big cities. Jacob-Moshe was one of them. And although his letters to his father contained much information about Zionist activities, particularly the progress made by the Labor Zionist groups, his father was not cheered. In this time of trouble and sorrow, rational thought and discussion would provide no answers. After Passover in 1919 Haim-Ber left town a second time and visited all the communities in our province to organize self-defense units. We found out later that his son was helping him and in spite of his handicap was conducting combat training exercises. About that time, a delegate from the self-defense unit of Tultshin came to our house with a letter from Haim-Ber to the wealthy men in our community soliciting their contributions for the purchase of a machine gun. The bearer of the letter told us that in critical moments, when the recruits of the defense units were discouraged and nervous, Haim-Ber raised their spirits with his song and dance routines and recitations. He even succeeded in organizing a choir and a tiny orchestra of fife and drum players, who gave concerts in camp. The messenger further reported that Haim-Ber gave Bible readings in Hebrew and in Yiddish translation and recited the verses of the contemporary Hebrew poets. These literary sessions often concluded with the singing of popular ballads, such as Bialik's "Between the Rivers Prat and Hidekel," Tschernichowsky's "Shadows are Cast," and even the Russian poet Lermontov's famous melancholy lyric "I set out all alone on my way. . ."

On the day after the festival of Shavuoth, the armies of Petlura broke into scores of small Jewish communities in the province of Podolia, and pitched battles took place tetween them and units of the Jewish self-defense forces. Haim-Ber employed Jacob's strategy in his battles with the hosts of his brother Esau (Genesis 30: 1-3) by dividing his forces in two parts: one, led by his son, made a frontal attack, while the other, under his own leadership, harassed the enemy from rear.

The first battle near Zemerinka was unsuccessful. It was told that then Haim-Ber shaved off his beard and almost all of his hair, leaving only a narrow tuft on his gleaming pate in the style of the Gaidamacks,* who were the most fanatical of Petlura's rabble. Attired in a Cossack uniform and with his unaccented Ukrainian speech, he was able to conduct negotiations and conclude treaties with Petlura's hordes and with the local peasantry.

When he learned of the latest target for a pogrom, he would

immediately inform the self-defense unit of that community to make all necessary preparations and would even send them assistance from his own reserves. In this way the Jewish units were able to seize the initiative and ambush the advancing enemy. The heroic exploits of several units of Jewish self-defense, especially those led by Haim-Ber, saved several Jewish communities from total destruction.

At dawn on the tenth of Tammuz (July), 1919, while the armies of Tutiunik were approaching our town, Haim-Ber stood on the railroad platform of the village of Turbov talking to one of the peasants who, like him, was waiting for the train. Haim-Ber was careful not to arouse the man's suspicion by inquiring too closely about events in the vicinity, but the man quite candidly disclosed that Tutiunik and his army were due to arrive in Vakhnovka and Zazov that very day to attack the Jews. Haim-Ber jumped as if struck by an electric shock and, forgetting where he was, yelled, "I, too, am going there!"

When he reached the outskirts of the town, the air was rent with the blood-curdling cries of the galloping, cheering horsemen waving their sabres over the heads of the fleeing victims. Cries of mercy and screams of horror filled the town square. In the alley leading from the main street to his house he found two corpses, shards and splinters of shattered window panes, smashed remnants of furniture and broken dishes. His wife Gittl was neither in the house nor in the cellar. Haim-Ber picked up a large basket and put into it the Sabbath candelbra and the silver chalice used for the Kiddush blessing of the sacramental wine. He also took his wife's new shoes and several expensive hides which were left after the liquidation of his shop. In his Cossack uniform, he looked just like all the other raiders with their spoils.

When he left the house he saw the older daughter of Mr. Feinerman being dragged away, kicking and screaming, by one of the Gaidamacks. Paralyzed at first with horror, Haim-Ber soon pulled himself together and knocked the rapist down with one powerful blow to the head. "Leave this girl alone!" he shouted. "She is mine along with these treasures I have taken from her house!" The soldier stunned by the blow to his head his nose bleeding profusely was bewildered and uncertain. When he tried to rise, Haim-Ber knocked him down again and quickly rushed the girl back to her house. He found her father and mother in the parlor, wounded and bloody, and two Gaidamacks trying to drag the younger daughter into the bedroom. Haim-Ber pulled out a revolver and shouted, "Jesus and Mary! You will both die on the spot if you as much as nick this young girl, who has bewitched me into making her a proposal of marriage!" The two rapists angrily demanded to know his army unit, but he was able to satisfy them that he was indeed one of them, and they left the house. He quickly cut off the girl's and her parents' tearful thanks and hurried them down to the hiding place in the cellar before the Cossacks or their companions could return. Without helping the wounded parents, and without disclosing his identity, Haim-Ber left by the secret exit to the alley.

At the house of Yosel the coachman he saw five Gaidamacks kicking two prostate Jews. Immediately, deftly and without raising his voice, he demanded that the Jews be given to him since these two "lousy yids" owed him money for a cow and calf which he had sold them only last week. "If they croak, I will be the loser", he said, quoting the proverb, "Dead men pay no debts, only the living do." The Gaidamacks proposed to barter the Jews for his sack of booty. The deal was made, and the killers left. The two Jews, Moshe the horse dealer and Haim-Itzy the baker, raised themselves up with difficulty and followed Haim-Ber into one of the houses, astounded by this gallant act of mercy on the part of such a "rightous" Gentile. They kissed his hands in deep gratitude.

Toward evening, when the battalion of rioting Cossacks left the town, an enraged and embittered Haim-Ber returned to his home. In his disguise even Gittl didn't recognize him, and she began to scream that a bandit had broken into her house to kill and loot. When he begged her to keep quiet and she heard her husband's voice issuing from this horrible apparition, she fainted. Haim-Ber caressed her forehead and revived her with a drink of cold water. Then Gittl burst out crying and informed him that the silver candlesticks, the silver chalice, and valuable furs were stolen. He replied tearfully, "A sacrifice, Gittl, a sacrifice — for the lives of our Jewish brethren! An atonement Gittl, an atonement: these valuable objects were lost and two Jews were saved!"

When I visited Russia in 1932, I saw him again in the city of Berditschev. His face had shrunk, his stature was bent and the penetrating gaze of his eyes was gone. His shoulders, which had been broad, were narrowed, and he was stooped. The old Haim-Ber told me that soon after the second pogrom in our town, the Jews of all surrounding communities were determined to defend their lives with arms and to avoid disgraceful death in some cellar or loft. "To die honorably" was the slogan. A Jewish military division of some 300 men, including some Jewish members of the Red Army, was organized. The men were well equipped with rifles and grenades. Jacob Moshe was one of the leaders. During a clash between a detachment of the Makhno Army, Jacob-Moshe had fallen on the battlefield. Gittl overcome with grief, died a few months later. Listening to Haim-Ber, I understood that the loss of his wife and son had taken away his desire to live. Later, friends told me that on the anniversary of their deaths Haim-Ber led the congregation in prayer. Then, once more he stood erect, his eyes blazing with the passion of revenge, his shouted pleas to heaven striking awe into the attentive audience. Afterwards, the people pointed to him and said: "The ministering angels in Heaven echo his pleas for mercy; Hossanah!"

Reb Nathan the Talmud Teacher

His wide forehead deeply creased, his beard and mustache thickly laced with grey hair, his body emaciated, his eyes running, coughing chronically — a sickly man was our Talmud teacher, Reb Nathan. He was not a strict disciplinarian. He allowed his pupils to run around during recess periods and began each lesson with light conversation. Yet, he insisted that his students realize the evil of idleness and the absolute good of diligent study. Even when he scolded us, we believed in the inherent goodness of his heart and his love for every one of us.

In the late autumn, the streets were muddy and the house cold. The shirt-waist under his kaftan could not warm his aching body. He coughed incessantly, sneezed profusely, his eyes running, his spittle dripping down on his long beard. Reb Nathan would then ask Breindl, his wife: "Breindl, a glass of hot tea, maybe? Or a hot potato, what?

When Breindl brought him a hot potato, which was still wet from the boiling water, the students contained their natural desire to prattle, and followed his chewing with interest and curiosity. In appreciation of their cooperation in keeping quiet during this interruption, Reb Nathan rewarded them with a story from the "Aggadah" (narrative portions of the Talmud) or Midrash (homoletic commentaries on portions of the Pentateuch). The children listened attentively. They gazed lovingly at his face, which suddenly glowed with brightness and warmheartedness. For fifteen to twenty minutes the teacher and his pupils were transported from the world of reality, which was full of toil and trouble, poverty and sickness, to an imaginary realm of light and joy. The heroes of his tales came alive with every new adventure. The festive air of a holiday filled the room. At the end of the story

Reb Nathan turned serious and resumed the lesson of the day with increased zeal, as if he regretted having wasted time on such vanities. The pupils began to sway to and fro in tune with the teacher's intonation of text and with a heavy heart continued to study the subject matter at hand. Out of love and respect for their teacher they reluctantly left the fascinating world of the "Aggadah" and immersed themselves in the intricate difficulties of the "Halakhah" (legal sections of the Talmud). The humming and chanting that rose from the students filled the room with a pleasant aura.

Reb Nathan was not a Hasid (follower of a religious movement stressing enthusiasm in worship) nor one of the antagonists of Hasidism. He criticized the former for neglecting intensive study of Talmud and their opponents for their dreary and monotonous way of worship. Although not endowed with a good voice, Reb Nathan loved to sing. He was a devotee of well-known cantors and was well versed in their versions of traditional chants. When he warmed up with a glass of hot tea he would ask the youngest student, Itzikl, who was a member of the synagogue choir in the city of Vinnitza, to sing "Like a shepherd mustering his flock", or "May they all come to worship Thee" (excerpts from the High Holiday prayers). Itzikl's rendition pleased him very much and he lovingly pinched his cheek in gratitude.

Breindl was a pious and virtuous woman. All of her neighbors were her friends. She did not have a single enemy in the entire community. Many of the town's women used to admire Breindl for her ability to cure all sorts of ailments. She was skilled in the treatment of stomach sickness using certain herbs she believed had medicinal value. Breindl was at her best, however, in removing the effects of the "evil eye". Children in particular were subject to this "sickness", which had no apparent cause but whose parents believed that it came from someone who had put "the evil eye" on the child. Breindl used to put her hand upon the head of the afflicted child, whispering certain incantations and suddenly her subject felt much better. She also taught the mothers how to relieve their children's sufferings caused by an "evil eye". The women followed her instructions and were sure that the effect of the "evil eye" had slipped away. Breindl could cure many ills save her own frequent aches and pains.

Reb Nathan loved his wife dearly and was always affectionate. There were no quarrels nor recriminations in their household.

I remember one day when Breindl took sick. Reb Nathan acted as if his world had come to an end. He was utterly incapable of teaching when his beloved wife was lying in the adjoining room sighing and writhing with pain. He could not keep his mind on the lesson, which was obvious to his sympathetic pupils when they noted the beads of perspiration which broke out on his face in the effort to pull himself together. Haim, the eldest of our group of students, who was capable of studying on his own, had risen and declared convincingly, on his own behalf and on behalf of all the students and their parents: "Please, Reb Nathan, take time off to take care of your sick wife, and with God's help she will recover. Do not worry about our being idle or wasting time. We hereby promise to review the lesson at home".

The whole group (which was 14 in number, including me) got up and left the room. After a while, Haim's mother came to the Heder (literally, room, also traditional school), found Reb Nathan sitting at his wife's bed caressing her hair. At once she, who was in her youth an experienced nurse, took charge of the situation: She fixed the curtain which divided the bedroom from the classroom, brought into the house an armful of logs and a small bundle of straw to light the stove, lit the stove, prepared a warm meal for the patient, patched up Reb Nathan's worn kaftan and washed a heap of laundry. The next day, when the pupils returned, they found their teacher in a good mood. When he saw his pupils seated in front of their open books, he put on his eyeglasses, coughed a bit and began to tell a story. He was so carried away by his growing enthusiasm that his eyes began to shine with youthful exuberance, and he jumped up ready to break into a dance. Haim drew near him and began to sing, joined by Itzikl with his high soprano. At first the tune was mellow, but it soon became boisterous, as one after another, the pupils joined in. Little Shelomo started "And He gave us a Torah of Truth", and his friends responded with "Once More, Once More — a Torah of Truth". The pupils were dancing in a circle around Reb Nathan, and Breindl and Sarah, Haim's mother, watched through an opening of the curtain, their faces beaming with joy.

Haim was the oldest in the group and Itzikl the youngest. Haim, a tall lad of fourteen, an exceptionally warmhearted boy, commanded the respect and admiration of the entire group of Reb Nathan's Talmudic students. In our eyes he was a young man worth emulating and his word for us was law. Haim's parents, honest middle-class merchants, made for their son the proper suits and gave him enough spending money. Haim would treat us occasionally to a little ice cream and oftentime to a bite of "Halva", a sweet Turkish delicacy. Itzikl, on the other hand, was a slim and sickly boy, whose mother was a widow, struggling hard to make a living. Head erect and dressed in black, she presented a picture of gracious nobility. The people knew of her poverty, yet they dared not offer her charity. More than once she quoted from Proverbs: "A debtor is a slave to his creditor", and "He who hates gifts shall live", to those who had the temerity to offer her money or a gift. She spent her days and evenings sewing for the wealthy women in town, who fancied her work, yet haggled over the price. She never quarreled with them; always looked relaxed even when handling the house chores. Itzikl was a great help to his mother. He used to go to the city of Vinnitza in the middle of the month of Elul and return the day after the festival of Succoth. He was one of the best singers in the choir of the Great Synagogue, for God had blessed him with a sweet, high pitched voice. He brought home twenty-five rubles — a very respectable sum of money in those days. His older sister, Hannah, helped her mother with the sewing and with the delivery of the clothes to the clients.

But Itzikl was an ailing child. His stomach troubled him and he had to be on a special, strict diet. Once, while Itzikl recited his lesson, his head dropped on the table in a faint. Reb Nathan ran quickly for the bottle of brandy, poured some into the palm of his hand and began to rub Itzikl's forhead. When Itzikl came to, our teacher picked up the sick child and carried him to the doctor. He seemed to have regained the strength of his youth, for when the two older pupils offered to help him, he angrily ordered them to go back to the Heder and tell the other children to go to their homes. It was reported that Reb Nathan ran to the doctor and then to the apothecary to get the doctor's prescription filled. He took Itzikl home and nursed him for the rest of the day and night, refusing to heed the pleas of the widow that he should lie down to rest while she did the nursing. Thereafter, Reb Nathan gave Itzikl a drink made of milk, eggs and honey, called "eggnog", every morning, which the boy drank behind the curtain, so that nobody, not even his mother, should find out.

Reb Nathan's knowledge of worldly affairs, such as trade, commerce, literature, or any other phase of secular culture was extremely scanty. The nickname "Melamed" (literally, teacher; employed in Yiddish as a term of derision for an impractical person) suited him well. Yet he kept up with the news of the world, and particularly of the Jewish community. He hardly ever read a newspaper, but the letters of his son Yonah, who was a student in Vilna, were as detailed and accurate as the dispatches of a professional newspaperman, and they kept him informed about all major events worth noting. During our studies Reb Nathan seasoned our discussions of the text with aphorisms and parables, which served to emphasize the oppression of Jews in the Diaspora and their yearning for liberation and redemption from it. He felt that life in the Diaspora was senseless; it was high time to begin talking seriously about returning to the Land of Israel.

I remember that on the day before the festival of Shavuoth, when there were no classes, he came to visit my grandmother, who served him a plate of cheese "Kreplach".* Reb Nathan ate the delicacy with great relish, and at the same time delivered the following homily:

"We all know that these dainty things prepared by your grandmother, may she be rewarded with a good and long life, are called "Kreplach". Furthermore, you may remember that not so long ago, when I visited here, she served me something we call "knishes".* Occasionally, when I visit you on Sabbaths and Holidays, this woman of valor serves me "Kugel",* or "Kartoffel", which I love dearly. Let me inform you that when the people of Israel lived in their own land, in the Land of Israel — each man under his vine and under his fig tree — these delicacies were known as: "replach'", "nishes", "ugel", "artoffel", and their taste was like the taste of Manna from Heaven. But since the destruction of the Holy Temple and our exile from the Holy Land, the real taste of these things has dissipated. That is why we add the letter "K" to the names of those dishes (the letter "K", as a prefix, serves in Hebrew as the preposition "like"): not the real "ugel", "replach", etc., but something "like" them. Providence Itself is in exile together with its children, and even food which is made to taste deliciously loses its full flavor. Thus our life is not a full one until the day of redemption from the Diaspora.

That is how Reb Nathan expressed his Zionist views and transmitted them to us.

During the civil war in 1917-1918 and the pogroms that followed, the parents of Reb Nathan's pupils, who were mostly petty traders, realized that travelling through the villages was fraught with danger because bandits and robbers were roaming the highways, and peasants were looking upon the Jewish peddlers with a jaundiced eye. Money was scarce. People were worried. They sat quietly in their homes with grim expressions on their faces. Some were hungry, nibbling at dry, stale bread. The number of pupils in the Heder decreased. Reb Nathan sat in his house confused and depressed, wondering where his bread was coming from. In a few weeks the Heder was practically empty. Several of his pupils were making the rounds of the villages trying to forage a few pennies, a bit of wheat, barley or grits, some potatoes, or a chicken. Those who spoke Ukrainian well would bring to the homes of the peasants for barter footware, caps or underware, a few boxes of matches, a little salt in return for vegetables, potatoes, onions, cheese, and sometimes even a chicken.

Life was hard, and Reb Nathan would sit with bowed head thinking sad thoughts. For two weeks he had been idle. Some of his erstwhile pupils brought him some food, most of which he turned over to Breindl, pretending that he wasn't hungry.

One day Reb Nathan took his only two pillows and started out for the nearest village, hoping that he would find some peasants who would give him food in exchange for the pillows. He bypassed the church, reached the street of the wealthy, passed the apothecary, the post office, the house of the doctor hidden behind shade trees, and finally stepped out on the highway leading to the country farms. He walked slowly, breathing in the fresh air. The grass was soft and deep and there was silence all about. About half a mile beyond the town he heard footsteps behind him. He turned around and saw his pupil Haim, who reminded him of the danger involved in walking alone on the road and persuaded him to step into the home of the friendly Gentile woman, Mrs. Krasnosielsky, which was only a short distance away. Haim took the pillows from his teacher and together they approached the house of this good woman.

Mrs. Krasnosielsky was known as a friend of the Jews. Even though her sons joined the Gaidamacks and undoubtedly participated in looting Jewish stores, she was welcomed in those homes as heretofore. She always brought to her Jewish friends gifts of fresh fruit, vegetables, and dairy products, and spent some time in Grandfather's store conversing with him on matters of current interest.

When Reb Nathan and Haim entered her house they found the two sons sitting at the table eating and their mother serving them. The sons cast angry looks at the unwelcome guests, and one of them angrily snatched the pillows away from Haim, hit him on the head, pushed Reb Nathan, and ordered them to leave the house. The mother's pleas to leave her guests alone fell on deaf ears. While Reb Nathan and his pupil stood in the center of the room bewildered and speechless, the elder son, who was dressed in an army officer's uniform, gave vent to his anger by attacking them, and kicking them out of the house. The gentle mother followed her guests into the yard and led them toward the stable, where she hitched a horse to a small wagon, in which she deposited two sacks of potatoes, a basket of eggs, and a pitcher of sour milk. When the three took their places in the wagon, ready to go, shots were heard. Her two sons, who were barring the way at the gate, pointed their guns and shouted: "If you, mother, transport those two "Zhids" (a derogatory term for Jews) you'll be bringing to town two corpses, because we'll shoot them dead here to show you that such people are not to be treated like decent human beings!" The woman realized that she had no choice but to ask the two to get off the wagon. Yet she loaded some of the food on Reb Nathan's and Haim's shoulders and apologetically asked them to go. But the sons were not satisfied. They pulled the sacks, the basket and the pitcher away from the two Jews and began to bombard them with potatoes and eggs. The teacher and his pupil were joined by the woman in screaming and wailing. Reb Nathan and Haim were felled by the barrage, which was followed by a hail of stones and loud guffaws of laughter on the part of the highly amused aggressors. Frightened and bewildered, their faces bruised, Reb Nathan and Haim dragged along to town.

After this incident the Talmud teacher changed radically. He frequented the meetings of the young people in town and planned with them the organization of self-defense units in the event of a pogrom. He joined the "apostate" Kunis in soliciting contributions from the rich men in town for the self-defense fund.

One night a group of marauders attacked the slum houses in a side alley near the public baths. No one saw that two of them entered Reb Nathan's house. He was lying in bed awake, and in the gloom of night saw two men armed with rifles approaching him. Breindl, who was also awake filled the still night air with blood-curdling cries. The men dragged Reb Nathan out of bed and knocked him down, kicking him in the ribs and pulling him by the hair of his head and beard. Under Breindl's mattress there was a little sack of copper coins, which she surrendered to the robbers. But they were not satisfied with this meager yield and lit a candle to keep looking for hidden heirlooms of silver and gold. Breindl, in her mortal fear, helped them find the silver Kiddush* cup, used for reciting the blessing over wine, the Sabbath candlesticks, the Hanukkah menorah* and the silver tableware which they had received as a wedding gift. Just before they left the house Reb Nathan recognized, in the light of the candle, the two sons of Mrs. Krasnosielsky.

For many days Reb Nathan lay in bed with his face to the wall. His pupils took turns watching over him. The doctor came daily to change his bandages. Gradually, he began to regain his strength. On Lag BaOmer (a minor festival dedicated to teachers and scholars) his pupils took him out to the woods for a bit of fresh air. They sat him down on a blanket against a tree and watched him with great love and respect. Reb Nathan caressed his beard with trembling hands, looking with admiration on the trees and shrubs. With tear-filled eyes, he observed his beloved students and began to expound his views about the Jewish problem. He told us of the Land of our Fathers, about the prophets who hallowed it with their divine visions, about the rebellion of Bar Kochba against the Roman legions in 132-5 C.E. (which is traditionally commemorated on Lag BaOmer) and the Ten Martyrs who gave their lives for the sanctification of God's Name (one of them was the saintly Rabbi Akiva, the spiritual mentor of Bar Kochba). He reviewed the bitter centuries of the exile, the massacres of 1648, 1882 and

1903 in the Ukraine, concluding that the recurring, endemic hatred of the Jew in the Diaspora proved that we must return to the land of our Fathers. In the meantime we must not submit passively to pogroms but organize our own self-defense to protect our lives and our property and to enhance our self-respect and our honor. The injunction in the Talmud bids us to kill the ones who are about to kill us. While killing is an abomination, saving one's life is a thou shalt do commandment. His weak voice rose in intensity and his eyes sparked with courage. When he finished talking, Haim stood up and began to sing the "Hatikvah" (an early Zionist hymn, now the national anthem of the State of Israel). We all stood up, and even Reb Nathan managed to rise, helped and held up by two students. While singing the verse "our eyes are turned to Zion", Reb Nathan must have thought he had heard the sound of horse hoofs approaching. He uttered "oy", his knees gave way and he fell dead of a heart attack. The students took off their "small talisses" (a small white "pancho", with ritual fringes in the four corners, worn under the street clothes by orthodox Jewish males) and covered their teacher's body. The younger pupils burst out crying. Haim quieted them down, and in tremulous, yet hope-filled voices we continued the refrain of the song: "our hope is not yet lost — our ancient hope. . . ."

Yosel the Coachman

Yosel the coachman leaps up to the driver's seat and grasps the reins firmly. With an air of great authority, he looks back to see if the passengers are seated in their assigned seats, and if the baggage is securely bound with ropes to the back of the coach. He casually observes the friends and relatives who have come to bid farewell to his passengers, and finally takes off with a snappy flick of his whip. An experienced driver, Yosel guides his horses slowly and cautiously through the narrow streets; but once on the highway outside of town, he whips his horses into a brisk trot with a shout and a whistle. The coach moves swiftly along a curved road bypassing the forest and quickly makes its way to the railroad station in the village of Turbov, about 12 miles from our town. Since there is a morning and an evening train, Yosel makes the trip twice a day. In the winter in snow storms and in heavy rain, when the mud is knee deep and the wheels get stuck in mire or sink in puddles of murky water, there is danger of the baggage coming loose and scattering, and Yosel makes only one trip a day.

Yosel, a tall, brawny Jew, stands erect, his face ruddy, his huge, calloused hands capable of the hardest work. People respect him for his courage and integrity: He says what he has to say without flattery or sycophancy. He speaks harshly even to his affluent passengers when they are tardy or when ordering them off the coach at rough points. They don't mind it — it's for their own good.

On Sabbaths and festivals, days of peace and relaxation, Yosel greets everyone good naturedly, adults and children alike, with a broad smile and a "Good Shabes", or a "Good Yomtev" (Sabbath and Holiday greetings). He sometimes plays with the children in the yard of the synagogue and pinches their cheeks, affectionate to all.

At home Yosel treats his two daughters and son with tenderness and kindness. He hugs them and kisses them often, and tells them tall tales about the wide open fields and the thick woods, where brave men fight desperate bandits, and smart, experienced horses follow the trail unfailingly without a guiding word or goading whip from the driver. Yosel pays special attention to the eldest, Mordecai, his only son, a tall lad with a round face, a full head of black curls and eyes that reflect his inner courage. On Saturday nights he spends a long time with the boy in the stable, explaining horses' anatomical features, their habits and peculiarities, and the art of coachmanship. In the summertime, when Yosel returns from the station of Turbov, father and son mount their horses and gallop off toward the setting sun. After the ride they rest in a cornfield and have some conversation. Mordecai listens respectfully to his father's instructive talk, but does not hesitate to correct contradictions in his father's statements. Yosel overlooks his son's lack of respect, gratified by the boy's alertness and intelligence.

After Mordecai grew up, he began accompanying his father on trips. In his son's presence the father tried not to berate his passengers or swear when the horses stumbled on rocks or clods of dried soil and caused the coach to lurch or skid. From time to time he would entrust the reins to him. Seeing the boy's bulging muscles straining to brake the eager animals, he felt assured that Mordecai would find his way in this uncertain world when the time came. Yet, as much as he took pride in his son's diligence and devotion to work, he regretted his lack of Jewish learning. Beside rote recitation of a few daily prayers and donning the phylacteries, the boy knew nothing. When Mordecai attended heder*, the teacher complained that he was not paying attention to the lessons — his mind was on other things. Yosel hoped that his son would ultimately master the art of translating portions of the Pentateuch, but it was not to be. Mordecai's sole interest was in horses and wagons.

One cloudy autumn day, the wagon was dragging along laboriously on its poorly lubricated axles. The horses pulled with all their strength, but the coach sank in the mud. Yosel whipped and whipped the horses but they could not budge the carriage.

Mordecai, who ordinarily dared not offer advice or criticism to his father in the presence of passengers, jumped up from his seat, and in an unequivocal, loud voice shouted: "Stop, Father!" He asked the passengers to descend and help pull the coach out of the mud. Yosel saw the passengers carry out his son's orders, lending a hand or a shoulder. With a combined effort they managed to free the mired conveyance and calm the heaving, foaming horses. Mordecai sat down again next to his father and looked at him to see whether he was angry. Yosel burst out laughing and so did the passengers, who stayed in a good mood all the way to the station. From then the bond of love between father and son was stronger than ever.

Soon Yosel acquired a "droshky" (one horse hansom). "It's all yours", he said to Mordecai, "a carriage for three passengers! From today you are a coachman on your own!" To and from the railroad station, Mordecai waved his whip with a flourish, and turning his head from time to time, smiled at his three passengers. Mordecai became a young man of substance.

To please his father Mordecai hired a teacher once a week to instruct him in Bible and in reading and writing Russian. He made great strides in his studies, and after three years, learned so much that the people dubbed him "the erudite coachman". His eagerness to learn affected his father. People began remarking that Yosel was taking lessons from his son's teacher and trying to read the "Ein Yaacov" (a popular anthology of Midrashic tales and commentaries).

Mordecai was exempted from military service and granted the coveted "Blue Certificate" because he was an only son. In Berditchev, the provincial capital, where he was investigated and examined before his deferment, he met young men his own age who were members of the "Bund" (Jewish Socialist Alliance). They initiated him in the esoteric ideologies of the various socialist factions. He spent about two months in the city, and met many students, men and women, Jews and Gentiles, who were preoccupied with the coming of the socialist revolution. He fell in love with Sonia, a young Gentile woman, and wooed her ardently, but to no avail. It was a difficult time for him. Before leaving the city he went up to her room to say good-by. Sonia berated him for coming without an invitation; "Filthy zhid (Jew)", she yelled, "get out of here!" Tired and hurt, he walked the streets, debating whether to return home or stay in the city and try to fathom how and why the plague of anti-Semitism had struck even the ranks of the socialist intelligentia. He must speak to these people, meekly or harshly; he must find out why Sonia called him the abusive "zhid". If those who prate about the ideal of human equality are capable of such gross prejudice, then his friends from "Zeire Zion", the Zionist Youth Organization, are right in maintaining that there is no prospect for a normal Jewish life in the Diaspora. Mordecai was troubled by dire premonitions about the welfare of the Jews after the Revolution. If even a girl like Sonia, who pretends to believe in the socialist ideal of total equality among races and religions, treats him with contempt, probably these "enlightened" Gentiles would prove more of a menace to Jews in critical times than the simple illiterate masses. Apparently, endemic hatred of the Jews had blinded even the eyes of the socialists.

The next day Mordecai drank his cup of hemlock in one gulp. He met his friend Stephan in the company of Sonia. This Stephan had been friendly with Mordecai, who helped him distribute revolutionary literature among the Jewish population. When Mordecai put out his hand in greeting, Stephan said angrily: "Leave Sonia alone, you filthy zhid! Go chase your own kind!" Mordecai knocked him down, Sonia screamed for help, and Mordecai was arrested and stayed in jail for a week, until his father came and bailed him out.

About a month after Mordecai returned home, still under the cloud of his bad experience in Berditchev, war broke out, and he was drafted with all the other "Blue Certificate" holders. After three months of basic training, he was being sent by train to the front. Travelling over the familiar fields of Podolia, he thought of home, his coach, and his friends. From the familiar landscape he knew he was nearing Turbov station. He made his way to the door of the car, gave it a push and hurtled out like a stone. Unhurt from the fall, he easily made his way to his father's house, but hid in the stable until evening. When his father came home they decided that he should not stay at home. That same evening Mordecai went to the house of Yavdokha, in whose cellar he fell soundly asleep. Yavdokha agreed to shelter him overnight on condition that he return to the army after seeing his family, not that she didn't hate the Tzar and his generals, but she felt that an able bodied young man like Mordecai ought not hide in a hole like a coward. Mordecai assured her that it was not fear that made him desert but a sudden yearning to see his family again. Yosel persuaded the local doctor to issue a certificate saying that Mordecai had hurt his leg when he accidently fell from an open window in the railroad car. He was sent back to his army unit, spent a year on the battlefield, and was decorated for bravery. Subsequently, he was taken captive by the Austrian army.

In the barracks for the prisoners of war he became friendly with one of the guards, an officer, who told him about his childhood in Vienna, his orthodox Jewish parents, especially his mother, a piano teacher who refused to receive pupils on the Sabbath. He recalled Russian and Polish Jews who were ardent Zionists visiting their home; some were close friends of Theodore Herzl, the founder of political Zionism. The officer taught Mordecai to read and write German. Ultimately, he mastered the language to the point that he could read Zionist literature and other books of Jewish interest in German. Among the prisoners of war was a young Hebrew writer from the city Zhitomir. They soon became intimate friends. In the months of captivity, Mordecai began to understand clearly what a precarious state Jews were living in.

The war came to an end and Mordecai returned home. Yosel, although overjoyed to see him, immediately recognized a great change in his son. His face was thin, his body had become lean, his eyes were sad, and his speech was slow and hesitant; his whole manner reflected alienation and reserve. Yosel worried. When his daughters were out of the house and his wife busy in the kitchen, he sat down at the edge of Mordecai's bed to talk with him.

"What of your future?" he asked.

Mordecai, uncertain, looked at his father and replied: "Father, no more horses and no more coaches. . ."

Yosel was astounded by such a categorical reply. This was not the same Mordecai who used to gallop on his horse like a cossack, who, he had hoped, would inherit his place on the driver's seat. "What will you do?" he finally asked.

"I will go to Palestine", Mordecai answered. Yosel apparently unable to digest his son's answer, did not reply. "To the land where the Patriarchs lived and died," Mordecai explained, "the land where a new Jewish life is being born!''

Yosel bewildered, sighed deeply. Tears appeared in Mordecai's eyes; he rose and embraced his father, and hugged him with all his strength. Mordecai gave his father a long lecture on Zionist ideology. Yosel did not quite understand the intricacies of his son's philosophy, but he felt better. Mordecai had convinced him that he had made the right decision. Yosel left the room still confused but reasurred that the intimate bond between father and son had not lessened.

In November 1917 news reached us of the revolution in Moscow and Petersburg. The reaction was ecstatic. Good times will come for the myriad inhabitants of this vast land. Brotherhood and friendship will reign supreme among men. Jews even believed that, at last, the animosity between them and their neighbors would vanish. In the same month we received news of the Balfour Declaration, in which the British pledged support for the establishment of a Jewish national home in Palestine. Our hearts were gay, there was no end to our rejoicing. Mordecai was busy every day, attending meetings, debating with members of the "Bund", and making speeches about the sacred duty of redeeming the Land of Israel at this propitious time. Yosel was dizzy from his son's sudden preoccupation with public affairs. He asked many questions and received clear, simple explanations, which he would quote, as best he could, to his passengers. The latter were truly amazed at Mordecai's metamorphosis: The simple, jolly young coachman had sprouted the Samsonic locks of an intellectual.

Too soon, however, the intoxicating "honeymoon" of recent events led to a sobering aftermath. The masses awoke from their heady dreams of peace, prosperity, and universal goodwill. Their disillusionment distilled into growing anti-Semitism, with which they had been indoctrinated for many generations. Hatred of the Jews turned increasingly into acts of aggression and violence. The members of the "Black Hundred", anti-Semitic intellectuals, were inciting the common people against the Jewish population. The establishment of local Soviets, which included some Jews, served as proof for the "turncoat" peasant revolutionaries that the Jews sympathized with the Communists. Jew baiters found a fertile field for their sinister activities. The situation of the Jewish people grew worse from day to day.

One cold, cloudy day Yosel, who was ill, sent his son to take five passengers to the railroad station. As the coach neared Turbov, shots were fired from the bushes. The horses panicked, and Mordecai, who was trying to rein the frightened animals, did not notice four men surrounding the coach. Two robbed the passengers of their boots and money, and the other two ransacked their baggage. When the bandits saw that the loot was meager, they took out their anger by beating the passengers with the butts of their rifles. Mordecai whipped out his army revolver, shot once over the head of the gang leader, and then directly at the one who was about to slash a passenger with his sabre. Meanwhile, two peasants working nearby heard the commotion and came to investigate. They, too, joined in beating the Jews. A full battle developed; two bandits and three Jews were killed, including Mordecai.

When Mordecai's body was brought to town, Yosel let out a horrible shriek and fainted. He mourned his son for many days. Then one day he put on his heavy winter coat, said good-by to his wife and daughters, and left town. Many tales reached us later of Yosel's feats in fighting outlaws. He had organized a band of Jewish fighters to harass Petlura's forces from the rear, as they committed more and more atrocities against Jews. It was also related that Yosel and his brigade had robbed a rich estate owner of a bundle of 100-ruble notes and distributed them among the self-defense committees of Kremenchuk and Yelisavetgrad; these two cities' volunteer security police, consisting mainly of Jews, ultimately brought the pogroms to an end. A blacksmith's son from the town of Zazov testified that Yosel burned down the houses of peasants who were known pogromists. Then we heard that Yosel had burst into a saloon in one of the villages, disarmed and beat up some men who were posing as soldiers of the Red Army, and took their leaders to the Red Army headquarters. When Yosel's escapades became generally known, he was arrested by the communist militia of Vinnitza and charged with counter-revolutionary activity. During the trial it was disclosed that he was fighting Gaidamacks, the enemies of the Soviets, and trying to avenge the murder of his only son. He was released. On his way home he developed a cold and high fever. Yosel was seriously ill.

When the local rabbi came to visit him, Yosel told him that he had taken a vow at his son's grave to avenge his death twenty fold. He figured that he had killed at least twenty men from the gangs of Sokolov, Tutuinik, and Attaman Gulick. But more important, he had saved scores of Jewish wayfarers and town dwellers from certain death. He remarked that as long as he rallied his colleagues with the battlecry "May my soul perish with the Phillistines!", they were inspired to struggle heroically for the honor of their people. After every encounter with the enemy he recalled his son's tireless efforts to encourage Jews to emigrate to Palestine. When he finished his "Viduy"*, the confession before death, he took out a little sack filled with paper money from under his pillow and handed it to the rabbi. He asked him to promise to use the money for the support of self-defense forces in Jewish communities. He asked, also, that one of the projected fighting units be named for his late son. The rabbi promised the dying coachman, in a voice choked with tears, that he would faithfully carry out his last will.

Yosel breathed his last breath in a spirit of innocence and sanctity. All the people in town came to his funeral, and every male Jew present recited the "Kaddish"* in tribute to a proud Jewish fighter, who gave his life for his people.

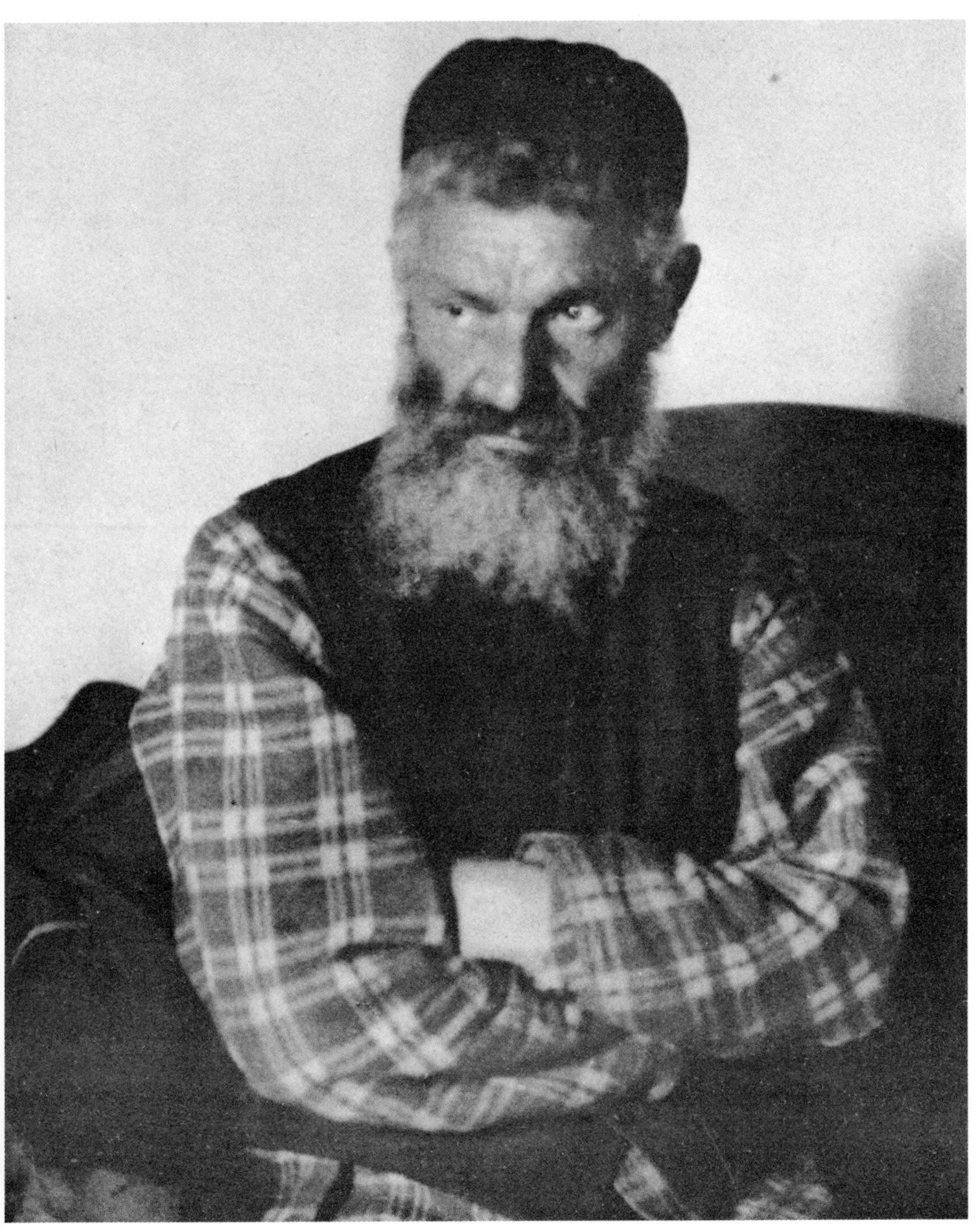

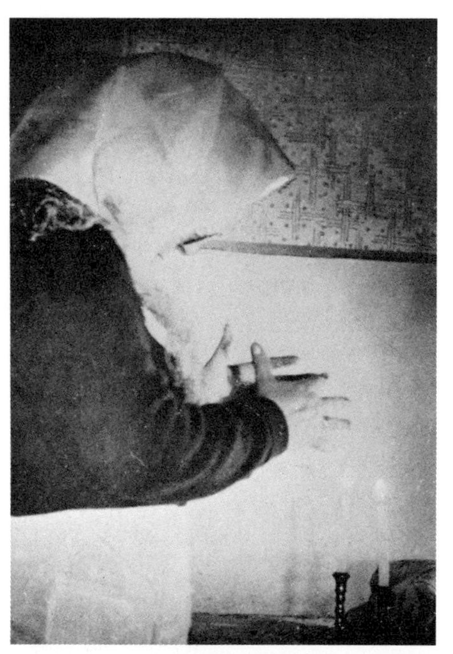

Kunis the Apostate

Isaac Borisovich Kunis was the chief bookkeeper of one of the two banks in our town. He was a vivacious individual with a sharp, penetrating look, dressed impeccably, clean-shaven, his shoes shined to high polish, an expensive cigarette smoldering in the corner of his mouth. He wore a pink tie against his white shirt, a wide cape that flared open in front, and a pair of gold-rimmed pince-nez. He looked, for all the world, like the proverbial "city slicker". Born and raised in Kiev, he spoke high style Russian and spiced his remarks with epigrams and metaphors. When the spirit moved him, he could recite poems by Pushkin, Lermontov, Nadson, and Simon Frug (a famous Russian-Jewish poet of the turn of the 20th century). After bank hours or on holidays and Saturdays, Kunis could always be found in the salons of wealthy people, whose daughters played the piano and read Russian novels. Evenings he would play chess with the Polish doctor, the Jewish apothecary, or the local priest. Occasionally, he would visit the home of the distillery owner, a rich Jew who had business with the local gentry. But on Saturday nights he would visit our home for a glass of tea and listen to Havdalah* and liturgic chants, such as, "Elijah the Prophet" and "Do Not Fear, My Servant Jacob". We children would sit at the table watching Kunis attentively trying to puzzle out this peculiar, sophisticated person from the big city who did not seem at all like a Jew. After Grandfather finished the traditional songs for Saturday evening, Kunis would look at him with an expression full of respect and tenderness and enthusiastically call out, "Yossiph Moisseyevich — Zamiechatelno!" (Joseph son of Moses — its wonderful!) He would move closer to father and they would have a long conversation. They spoke Russian, which was difficult for us to follow, but we understood enough to know that they were discussing current Jewish events, such as, the problems of the Society for the Diffusion of Culture and Education among the Jews of Russia, the speeches of the Jewish representatives in Duma (the parliament in the last decade of Tzarist Russia), the debates at the latest Zionist Congress and anti-Semitism. The conversation would be interrupted when the time came for us to go to bed. Kunis and father would come up with us to hear our bedtime prayers and say good night. Kunis would hug us and whisper unintelligible endearments in Russian, and then return with father to the parlor for more conversation and tea drinking. Father used to say that Kunis was a good man, a lover of mankind, who was trying to get to know his own people better.

When Kunis first came to town, people berated him for not attending synagogue on Sabbaths and festivals, and for walking about the streets bareheaded. They considered him an assimilated, apostate Jew. But when they learned that he was an expert in financial transactions, that he had dealings with big businessmen, and that when he lived in Kiev he was very active in Jewish communal affairs, they were willing to forgive his big city style. Later it also became known that he had refused to convert in order to be admitted to the university. (The Russian schools for higher learning limited the number of Jews to two percent; there were no restrictions for converts to Christianity). This made people respect him even more.

In the spring Kunis would walk in the woods and fields and enjoy the aroma of the early bloom and brilliance of the cloudless skies. He used to like to climb the only hill in the outskirts of town, which commanded a view of the fields, the valley and groves beyond the river. On occasion, he would come across groups of young people who held their clandestine meetings in the woods: Socialists, Zionists, nihilists, and other visionaries and dreamers. Some nights a group of these young adults would row a boat out on the river and sing revolutionary and romantic songs. Kunis loved to listen to Tcharna, the cantor's daughter, whose attractive face and radiant eyes made love blossom in the hearts of men. She would sing Frug's poem "Carry my soul into the distance of blue . . ." The depth of feeling conveyed by this poem, which bemoaned the fate of Jews, and the mystery which seemed hidden in Tcharna's soprano rendition of it awakened in Kunis a longing for fulfillment — a fulfillment that would only be found in redemptive work for his people.

These idealistic youths attracted Kunis, especially the bright-eyed, high-spirited Abraham. Kunis could listen to this talented young man speak about the Jewish problem for hours! "From the early days of modern anti-Semitism to the pogroms of Kishinev" (where mass murders of Jews occured in the spring of 1903), Abraham asserted, "whenever there were pogroms and massacres, the Russian intelligentsia were utterly oblivious. To this day they look upon the Jews as some exotic sect that calls on occult powers to undermine the existence of the non-Jew. Hatred of Jews is as old as the exile itself. Since the early Christians began accusing Jews of crucifying Jesus, Jew-hating has gone hand in hand with pagan conversion to Christianity. As long as Christianity tolerates it, anti-Semitism will prevail, even among people who are not religious zealots. Anti-Semitism is especially wide-spread among those opposed to changes in the social order. Their strategy is to divert attention from their own problems by inciting the masses against the Jews. Furthermore, they accuse the Jews of leading revolutionary movements, of plotting to overthrow the present regime. Today, when the socialists are struggling to seize power, they exploit the Jews as propagators of socialist doctrine, on the one hand, and incite the common people to fight Jewish capitalists, on the other. In every generation the Jews have been scapegoats for the sins of humanity. For centuries we have been the most despised and rejected people. There is no alternative but to defend ourselves by force. If all our wealthy Jews would help the Zionists organize mass migration to Palestine, buy land there, and unite our scattered and disorganized communities, we would be reborn. Only by building a new life in Palestine will we wipe out the stain of Jewish passitivity to persecution and raise a new generation proud of being Jews."

Listening to Abraham, Kunis' mind would be occupied with the "whys" and "wherefores" of his own failure to see the Jewish problem in this light. His friendship with Russian intelligentsia prompted him to disagree with Abraham's analysis. He found that most of his Russian friends held liberal and progressive views, and their conduct attested to a tolerant attitude towards Jews. On the other hand, he recalled certain incidents of hostility toward Jews. Even during his visits with gentile friends in Kiev, he heard occassional derogatory remarks. Were his encounters with tolerant non-Jews an exception to the rule? Reflecting on the problem he was conscience stricken; he could not understand why he had not become more involved with the affairs of his people. As encounters with Abraham and his colleagues developed into real friendship, Kunis became more critical of himself, wrestled with the problem of anti-Semitism, and found that his judgement of the state of the Jew was superficial and shortsighted. Eventually, he decided to atone for ignoring his people's destiny and letting himself be misled by the empty promises of Russian liberals.

In a conversation with my father, a Maskil,* he recalled attending the High School of Commerce in Kiev. In his class were only three Jewish students, admitted to the school after passing competitive examinations. One of them came from a small town. The Russian teacher mispronounced his name "Judah" deliberately to sound like the name of the traitorous apostle Judas Iscariot. Mouthing this despised name, her voice filled with poisonous hatred and her looks betrayed thoughts of vengeance against this scion of the "Christ killers". The Jewish boy would stand before her in abject submission, shaking in apprehension of the inevitable fate of one whose ancestors allegedly commited deicide. For three months he held out against harassment, then left school. Fair-haired Kunis' gentile looks and manner made him acceptable to his non-Jewish school mates, but still he could sense the deepseated hatred in the hearts of his teachers and classmates. Once he inadvertedly splashed a few drops of ink on the shirt of the boy sitting next to him. The latter hissed out between clenched teeth, "filthy zhid" (Jew); during the recess period several students surrounded him and beat him. His father, instead of discussing the problem at length with him advised him to suffer in silence and stick it out for the sake of a good education and a successful career. He followed his father's advice and ignored the constant stream of derogatory remarks and insults.

Kunis began visiting our home more frequently. Father would read and translate articles from the Hebrew periodicals Ha-Shiloah* and Ha-Tzefirah* for him; tell him about the experiences of the members of the "Second Aliyah"*; report discussions which took place at the World Zionist Congress; and for "homework" gave him copies of the Russian-Jewish weekly Rassviet. Kunis began to visit scholars and public figures, such as Reb Israel Kuzris, Jacob the Cantor, and Abraham-Joshua, the ritual slaughterer to discuss the Zionist ideology and program.

It was in that period that an intimate friendship developed between Kunis and me. For hours this man would sit with me, a boy of 12, urging me to recite Bialik's poetry and chapters from the prophets Isaiah, Jeremiah, and Amos. I would strive mightily to translate this material into crude Russian. Kunis would stand before me like a pupil before his teacher. Mouth agape, he moved from one chair to another, and rose again full of admiration for his "erudite" and "inspired" teacher.

Kunis discussed current events, also, with my sister, five years my senior, who attended Gymnasium* in Uman, and whose visits home were frequent. She, too, was active in Jewish affairs. Once he told her of his experiences with orphaned Jewish children who attended a private school. Kunis used to bring the children milk and crackers and, occasionally, distributed clothes among the more deprived ones.

Among the pupils of that famous school was a poor, blind girl. She had lost her sight when a band of gentile boys threw stones at her. Her parents brought her to Kiev to live with relatives, who enrolled her in this school. The girl, ten years old, listened attentively to the lessons and tried to memorize excerpts from Russian poets as well as from the Prophets and Psalms. Sometimes she would recite or sing verses of Isaiah in a strong voice, as if to impress her listeners with her conviction; at other times her voice was lower and uncertain, seeming to reflect her sorrow at being blind. Once she recited Bialik's "The City of Slaughter" (an ode in the prophetic style, in which this famous poet chastised his people for their abject submission to pogroms) — she shivered with excitement, punctuating the words with deep sighs, and finally burst into tears. Kunis befriended this unfortunate girl, brought her gifts, and taught her to play the balalaika. This little blind girl dreamed of settling in Palestine. "There the warm sun will heal my eyes," she would say. "The beautiful landscape and freedom from oppression will be a slave for my wounded spirit." But her dream did not come true. She was killed in a road accident, and Kunis mourned for her a long time.

While he was still learning to identify with the Jewish nationalist movement, war broke out. Life lost its zest and joy. When Jewish refugees from front communities began streaming into our town, Kunis gave of himself unstintingly to relief activities. He gave his apartment to a refugee family and moved in with his friend, the apothecary. When he spoke to his Gentile friends of the suffering of the Jewish refugees, they became greatly annoyed. Only Yavdokha, the beautiful young peasant woman who associated with the local intelligentsia, was sympathetic. Once she remarked that Jewish troubles in Russia stemmed from their rootlessness, from their not having a land of their own. Despite the centuries they had been in Russia, they were the first to suffer the consequences of social upheavals, because they were still the "Wandering Jews".

Kunis was filled with anxiety for the future. He spent sleepless, depressed nights pondering the fateful question: "What will tommorrow bring?"

Desertion from the front had begun. Renegade soldiers joined outlaws from the countryside in attacking travellers and inhabitants of isolated settlements. Kunis foresaw the seriousness of these incidents. He resigned from his position in the bank and began travelling from town to town in the provinces of Kiev and Podolia organizing war relief committees. In each town, he investigated the possibilities of recruiting young people for self-defense units. Returning from a meeting late at night in the city of Dimievka, he was waylaid by a gang which beat him up, emptied his pockets, and stole his overcoat. Shivering from cold, bruised, and in shock, he made his way to a friend's house in the center of the city. His wounds were bandaged, but it was discovered that he also had typhus. His friend nursed him, doctors attended him, and he soon recovered. During his convalescence he resumed his Hebrew and Zionist studies. When he was ready to return to his activities, he learned that Jews had been attacked in the streets, and that Jewish shops had been pillaged. The police had not interfered. The trouble lasted a few days until Jewish youth organized forces for a counterattack and drove the assailants away. Kunis held several meeting with the leaders of the group and enlisted their help in organizing self defense brigades in a number of communities.

In the city of Golovensk Kunis met an elderly Jew who had organized a self-defense force during the pogroms of 1905. This man told Kunis that the force had saved the Jewish community from a devastating pogrom. "If I do not take care of my own, who will?" thought Kunis. He decided that what the Jews of Golovensk did in 1905 could be done again. Jewish self-defense was the order of the day. It must be implemented at once. He must convince community leaders of it, and campaign vigorously among the working people and the youth.

Political events (German occupation, fall of the Kerensky regime, rise of Ukrainian militancy), one after another, accelerated the pace of the Revolution. When the Bolsheviks seized power and declared amnesty for all deserters from the Tzarists armies, civil war ensued. The Jews, hated by the Ukrainians for centuries, suffered a severe blow. Masses of murderers, smelling blood and loot, emerged from obscure places and flooded the countryside to the point of deluge. Extinction hovered over the Jewish communities as Petlura seized power in the Ukraine, declared war on the Red Regime, and threatened the Jews with massacres.

Kunis' wanderings brought about a vast change in his thoughts, feelings, and speech. Although he was not conscious of any change, his friends were. He still spoke broken Yiddish and read Hebrew with the help of interpreters, but he was now an exponent of Jewish nationalism. He made fiery speeches in synagogues and to youth groups, openly advocating resistance and, if need be, actual warfare.

Hundreds of Jewish communities were bearing the brunt of pogroms. Old men were beaten; women raped; bodies of the dead lay unburied in open fields and on roads. Kunis and his associates doubled their efforts. In the small town of Burchanovka, near Skvira, Kunis organized a unit of 52 fighters, among them 13 Jewish war veterans, 16 young Jewish artisans, and the rest local peasants. They defended the community for a few weeks; but when a Red Army unit arrived, the Ukrainians deserted to Petlura's army. These men, supposed erstwhile defenders, attacked Jewish homes at night, looted them and set them on fire, and then threw some of the people who lived in them into the fire. The report of this atrocity hardened Kunis' determination to resist. He established self-defense units in three more Jewish settlements and participated in their successful efforts to ward off attacks. He was fearless. For long hours he stood guard, rifle in hand, stars shining in the stillness of the night, comrades in arms by his side, and he imagined himself a true descendant of the Maccabees. Except with his protection, people could not sleep soundly at night. Self-defense seemed so obvious an answer that he started travelling again from town to town organizing more and more units.

When Kunis heard about the pogrom in our town, he rushed there. He found the whole community preparing to move to Lipovitz, 25 miles away. Thirty-six men had been murdered in the Gaidamack pogrom headed by Tutiuniuk. Among the casualties were four of his best friends, including my father. The houses and shops were left unlocked, since they had been thoroughly looted. The people were disorganized, the evacuation was unplanned and unsupervised: old men leaning on their canes, women wailing, and children running around aimlessly among the wagons loaded with salvaged goods. Some friendly peasants from nearby villages were begging them to return home, swearing "by Jesus" to protect them in the future. But the people had enough of such "protection". Kunis tried to dissuade the leaders of the community from leaving, but no one listened. When the exodus began, Yavdokha, the young peasant woman, showed him several carts, the owners of which stood ready to transport old people and children to Lipovitz. Kunis understood that Yavdokha was the initiator of the scheme; she had mobilized the peasants and their carts for the evacuation: twenty wagons to transport 245 Jews to Lipovitz.

Kunis would not join the refugees. He remained in town, visiting the empty houses and, especially, the homes of the old and sick who had stayed, despairing of their lives. He visited the cemetery with its new, common grave for the 36 martyrs. Brokenhearted, he returned to his room. His furniture was smashed, the bed overturned, the mattress ripped, his books torn and scattered, even windows broken. He walked to the priest's house. Six bloodsoaked Jewish youngsters were lying on the floor in one of the side rooms. The priest had saved their lives and hidden them in his house. Kunis went down to the cellar, which looked like a warehouse, so full of copper and silver utensils, pillows and blankets — remains of the property of the poor whom the priest had befriended and protected. Kunis told the priest of his wanderings and exertions, of the horrible atrocities committed in the Jewish communities. The priest wept. Kunis took leave of this humanitarian clergyman and went to see Reb Israel, the renowned scholar of our town.

The old man lay in bed scanning a book through his eyeglasses. He invited Kunis to sit down and immediately began speaking about the problem that had been bothering him: "I respect apostates who are erudite", he said. "Even though your knowledge of our religious sources is meager, I respect you for your sincerity and your readiness to defend the honor of our people. I see that doubts are corroding your consciousness. You have returned to your people, but it is difficult for you to accept the idea that this people is the Chosen People of God. I, too, find it hard to accept this doctrine, and my heart grieves to contemplate such an election for suffering and grief. What is the meaning of it? How long must we wait for the Messiah? What if he tarries for centuries? How many millions must be massacred?" Reb Israel was so disturbed that he began to shout and shudder until an attack of severe coughing stopped his speech. Kunis lifted the exhausted head from the pillow and cradled it in his arms. The coughing gave way to sobbing. Kunis kissed him and repeated: "How long, how long"? We learned of this touching meeting from Kunis' diary, which was found in a drawer of his desk a few days after he left our town forever.

Kunis rode a horse to the railroad station in Turbov. He had to get to his parents in Kiev. Near the village he was ambushed by four horsemen. They took his horse, but since they thought that he was a Gentile, did not molest him. On the train, as it was approaching the town of Kalinovka, he heard a child moaning. He turned around and saw a burly man beating a little Jewish boy to the amusement of the other passengers: "Little Jew, make the sign of the cross!" the man commanded loudly. "No, I cannot," cried the boy. "But you must, if you want to live!" shouted the man. "No, it is against my religion," muttered the boy. The man belted the boy's head again and again. The child's cries maddened Kunis so that he could not contain himself. He fell on the brute and wrestled him to the ground. When they were both down, Kunis pulled a penknife out of his side pocket and thrust it into the man's chest. The man began to yell: "Jesus Maria!" Kunis echoed, "Sh'ma Yisrael!"* Two young men approached with heavy clubs. One kicked the prostrate boy and the other clubbed Kunis on the head. He saw, as if in a dream, the blind girl from Kiev beseeching him not to give up. He made an effort to rise, succeeded in stabbing one more brute but a heavy clout fell on his head and he collapsed over the boy's body embracing him tightly. Clinging to each other, they succumbed to repeated clouts.

Their bodies were found in a grove near the station. The murderers had apparently cast the bodies out of the moving train. The Jews who were burying them saw an old peasant weeping near the cemetery fence. The old man testified to the horrible deed, committed before his eyes. He made the sign of the cross. "I thought I saw the roof of the railroad car open," he said, "and an angel from heaven descend and spread his wings over the bodies of the murdered man and boy, lying in tight embrace, wipe their blood, kiss their closed eyes and ascend upward to heaven. . ."

Hannah and Her Two Sons

There were five saloons in our town; the largest and most distinctive, located in the market place, was under the personal supervision of "the strong" Hannah. The saloon's clientele consisted of wealthy peasants from nearby villages and officials of the large estates, all with ready cash willing to spend it on food and drink. These customers were served large platters of sausages, smoked meat, pickled melons and vegetables, mixed pastries, and the best vodka and imported wines. They admired the young hostess Hannah, a tall, handsome woman, with two thick braids, a pretty mouth, and blue eyes, who dressed in black like a mourner. Everything about her spoke of energy, will, and resolution. The owner of the business was her father, a vigorous Jew, tall and well built, who, despite his obvious ailments, cast fear into any man who rubbed him the wrong way. Hannah spent much time in her private room adjacent to the main hall of the saloon. Save for working with her father on the budget late into the night, she would emerge only when one of the more prominent customers came in to pay his bills or seek advice on some important business matter; when one of the officials demanded that he be served his drink by the daughter of the proprietor; or when no one else could quiet an intoxicated customer. In such emergencies she would not hesitate to bring her strong arms and legs into the fray and distribute a few slaps and kicks. Her nickname "the strong one" was not for nothing — when she thrust her fist into the face of the troublemaker, the fracas ceased and the place returned to normal.

Hannah spent long hours in the saloon only on market days, when business was heavy. She would walk around the room shaking hands and smiling. When a particularly prominent guest was there, she would sit down at his table for a while and engage in polite conversation. She was, however, reserved in speech and gesture and always showed that she had self-respect, like an aristocrat who values her dignity and honor. She was well aware of the lascivious looks of some men, particularly the ones who had a bit too much to drink, but she ignored them, as if they didn't concern her.

Hannah separated from her husband three years after their wedding. She could not tolerate his obnoxious behavior: constant drinking, coarse remarks and ribald jokes, abominable manners, and loud voice like a braying beast. After a great deal of trouble and suffering, Hannah obtained a divorce and went with her twin sons to live with her father. During the first year of separation from her husband she was courted by some of the most eligible men in town. But they soon learned that Hannah was not an "easy catch". Her sons were small and required a lot of care. She was devoted to them and had no time or desire for flirtation, even with men whom she respected.

In time she set aside regular intervals for study, and made considerable strides in mathematics, natural science, history and Hebrew language and literature. Once a week she met with Shmuel-Leib, a middle-aged bachelor, who tutored her in all the subjects. Shmuel-Leib, well versed in classical literature and an accomplished flutist, was impressed with her achievements. To help her advance socially, as well as intellectually, he introduced Hannah to some of his friends — university students, wandering literati, and erudite laymen. Before long she became a member of the town intelligentsia, and gained distinction as an intelligent person. She developed skill in witty and sophisticated turns of speech, and amazed her listeners. After every session one of the men would walk her home, the most ardent of them was a Ukrainian engineer, who was bewitched by her elegance, youthful figure, and shining eyes.

One mellow summer evening Hannah took her two sons for a walk. As they were enjoying the beauty of the fields of wheat and barley, the delightful stretch of brook flowing in the shade of old trees, she was accosted by two men, one dressed in city clothes and bespectacled, and the other dressed like a farmer. The older of the two, speaking in a Moscowite dialect shouted: "Abominable witch, filthy Jewess, scabby slut, seed of that accursed tribe which is obstructing the advancement of the Ukrainian people;" and the other, talking in Ukrainian, yelled profanities in a voice filled with hatred. Hannah shuddered with rage but held fast to her little sons' hands, and restrained her anger. Suddenly the two men kneeled before her, changing their tune to amorous flattery, and tried to embrace her. Hannah taught them an object lesson with her clenched fists. She boxed their faces ferociously and beat them. Nevertheless, she returned home tense and worried, resolved to keep the matter secret. Her two sons, however, bragged about the incident to their friends, proud of their mother's victory over the two men.

Later, at a party in the home of her friend, the apothecary, she saw a man with a bruised face and bandaged ear sitting in a corner of the room. She immediately recognized him as one of the two she has thrashed that evening. He was none other than the "liberal" Gentile who babbled about granting equal civil and political rights to minorities, who praised highly the works of Jewish writers he read in Russian translation. A bolt of pain pierced her as she realized that many of the "friends" of the Jews were in reality their bitter enemies. In an ugly mood she left the party and returned home.

Hannah spent a sleepless night, troubled by the realization that even among the best Gentiles there were Jew-haters. She was all the more disgusted by the fact that these hypocrites who felt free to come to the apothecary's parties, gorge themselves on his food, and drink his wine, were plotting against her life and lives of her people. They were the agitators and demagogues who were ready to lead mobs of Russians and Ukrainians against innocent Jews. From that day she stayed away from the circles of Gentile intelligentsia. She tried to explain her attitude to the apothecary, but he ridiculed her suspicions. She argued with other Jews who had friendly relations with enlightened Ukrainians, but they, also, tried to assuage her anxiety with casual words of consolation. Even Schmuel-Leib, her teacher, refused to take her seriously.

In time Hannah began attending Zionist meetings, reading Zionist literature, and striking up friendships with active Zionists. Once she persuaded the wife of Haim Itzy, a devout follower of the hassidic rabbi of Sadigura, to permit her to be present at the monthly gathering of local Sadigura hassidim which took place in

Haim Itzy's house. Hannah was eager to see how the hassidim observe the *Seudah Shleshlt**, a festive gathering on Sabbath afternoons. It is the main monthly communion for hassidim. She listened to their songs, watched the changes of mood from melancholy to jubilation, and alone in her room, hummed the tune of the chant, "and redeem your people from exile". Little by little she came to the conclusion that the struggle of the Jewish people to preserve their physical survival and spiritual uniqueness must lead to the achievement of equal rights in the Diaspora and political sovereignty in Palestine.

At that time her personality changed radically. The saloon became an insufferable burden to her. The drunken customers disgusted her. Before long she and her two sons left town. The teacher of the town's Hebrew school visited Kiev in the fall of 1913, and reported that Hannah was a daily visitor to the courtroom of the trial of Mendl Bayliss. Mendl Bayliss was the defendant in an infamous "blood libel" trial. The whole civilized world was horrified at the accusation that this simple man had murdered a Gentile boy to bleed him for Jewish ritual purposes. Hannah was seen in the company of writers and community leaders, revolutionaries, press columnists, who were concerned with the false accusation of an innocent man. Hannah became friendly with one of the defense attorneys who took her to the theatre, concerts, and meetings of the underground. At times Hannah isolated herself and indulged in daydreams. She appeared chaste and refined, like a pious Jewess steeped in prayers. She read a great deal about Jews and Judaism, and was frequently seen in synagogues. Then, suddenly, the aura and manner of traditional Jewish feminine timidity disappeared, and Hannah emerged dressed in the latest fashion, her hair coiffered like an opera primadonna's. She acted like a daughter of an affluent burgher. Near the end of the trial, when the ludicrous and the intensely dramatic ran together in the confrontation between the prosecutor and the defense attorney, Hannah once again changed her life style. Hillel Movshitz, the rich storekeeper who went to Kiev for medical advice for his liver ailment, came back to Vakhnovka and reported that he had heard Hannah deliver a speech at a mass meeting in one of the synagogues. She was dressed in black, her head covered, and spoke with deep feeling about the anti-Jewish propaganda carried on by the reactionary groups, known as the "Black Hundred" to incite the masses of Russians and Ukrainians with the accusation that the Jewish religion calls for the ritualistic comsumption of Christian blood. She also spoke of the plight of the Jews in the "Pale of Settlement"*. Her sons, Hillel reported, were studying Jewish music and were particularly fond of Hassidic melodies. Both sons together with their mother devoted a great deal of time to the study of Jewish history and literature. Thus, we knew that it was a time of transition in the life of "strong Hannah".

When the war broke out Hannah returned to Vakhnovka. Her two sons were drafted into the army, and her father, who was too feeble to take care of the saloon, asked her to return to its management. With a heavy heart she served the customers, who, regardless of her dour disposition, showed her much affection. From time to time she would pay a visit to the priest, who was everybody's favorite, and talk about current events with him. He discussed Marxist theory in Leninist interpretation with her, Nietzshean philosophy, and the problem of anti-Semitism. This cleric, a seeker after truth, who overtly opposed the revolutionaries, apparently was a secret devotee of socialism. This sincere individual, whose heart bled for all oppressed people and who empathized with the suffering of the Jewish masses, was an inveterate reader of "subversive" literature. From time to time Hannah would have a discussion with my cousin, a man of deep feeling and an enthusiastic Zionist, who worked day and night for the Odessa Committee (a center of Zionist activity in Tzarist Russia"). She also talked to my father about the great difficulties of putting Zionist theories into practice; because the implementation of the Zionist program called for strenuous effort as well as idealism.

The revolution of 1917 brought in its wake civil war and the destruction of Jewish settlements. When Hannah used to visit my father she would always meet me with a smile. On her last visit I noticed that her smile was haunted with sadness. Hannah's stormy nature gave her no peace, and again she disappeared from her father's house. We learned from reliable sources that she went to Moscow. It was a long and difficult trip, through primeval forests and isolated settlements; for regular train service was erratic and uncertain in those troubled days. Her occasional letters to some of her friends in town always posed the same fateful question: Which is the road to salvation — Zionism, which seemed beset with innumerable problems, or Communism, which promised to liberate all nations, including the Jews? Apparently in one of her vacillations she had decided to join the Bolshevik party. Later we received news that she had enlisted in the Red Army in one of the cities of Central Russia. This is how it happened: In her persistant wanderings she had met a Bolshevik commissar, a Jew from one of the towns in our province, whom she had known previously as a Zionist. After much argument with him she was convinced that only in the ranks of the Bolsheviks could she realize her goal. She was certain then that the whole world was destined to come to judgment, and that the only underlying moral of the Bolshevik ideology would stand the test of history.

In the meantime her sons had returned from the front. One of them had lost the sight of an eye. It was not easy to track down their mother, who roamed the country with her Red Army brigade, fighting the reactionary White Army and Ukrainian nationalist forces of Petlura. Her sons enlisted in the Red Army brigade of which she was the political commissar. Hannah dressed in a leather jacket, revolver attached to her wide leather belt; bursting with energy and hope, she labored to plant in the hearts of her charges a fanatic faith in the future of the Bolshevik regime. Her exploits as a propagandist and a soldier were well known in our town. We had heard from reliable sources that, in addition to her regular duties Hannah was searching for the enemies of our people who were responsible for the pogroms. Did not the banners of Golub's army carry the legend: "Death to the Jewish harlot — Hannah! Beat her Jewish brethren and save the Ukraine!" This was the best proof of their hatred for this woman, who was fighting them with all her strength. When her sons joined her, the three of them carried out inquiries, thorough investigations among the prisoners of war, to discover who had benefited from Jewish favors and repaid the kindness with pogroms. Her Jewish colleagues in the Red Army supplied her with lists of the names of known anti-Semites from their home communities, and Hannah used those lists to bring the culprits to justice. Military justice was swift and merciless. It was rumored that 122 instigators of pogroms had been unmasked, sentenced to death and executed.

Hannah arrived in the city of Vinnitza during a bitter battle between the Reds and their enemies. The hard, perilous life of the army had greatly altered this remarkable woman's appearance: Her braids were stained with gray hair, her face was pale and her body lean; only her eyes still sparkled with courage. Some of our townspeople talked with her in Vinnitza, the headquarters of one of the most militant Soviet brigades in the Ukraine. She asked questions, especially about the Halutz units (Zionist pioneer youth) which were forming then in the larger Jewish communities to prepare their members for life in a kibbutz* in Palestine. She told Shmuel-Leib, her former teacher, that although her heart was in the East, she would remain in the West (paraphrasing a famous poem by the medieval, Spanish-Hebrew poet Rabbi Judah HaLevi). She did not have the patience to wait for the Zionist solution of the Jewish Problem. She was, also, anxious, to prove to the world that Jews know how to fight for their honor, that they also strive for civil rights, equality, and freedom. That was why her place was among the Bolsheviks, who were shedding their blood to establish a new order of free men. Schmuel-Leib also related that Hannah used to take contemplative walks by herself, even in dangerous areas.

After a while Petlura's forces got the upper hand and won some impressive victories. Pogroms spread to many Jewish communities. The number of casualties mounted from day to day. A refugee from our town reported to Hannah the murder of her father on the day of the pogrom. He was killed by an officer with long thin hair and a scarred face, who with his gang made shambles of the saloon. Hannah immediately recalled him as the man who had accosted her on her walk on a summer evening some years ago. Telling her sons what happened, she felt as if she were choking. Rumors began to spread about the connections between the Red Army and the Jewish self-defense units, which presumably explained why the latter succeeded in repelling pogroms in a number of communities. It was also reported that the thin-haired, scarred officer had fallen in one of the fights killed by the "notorious" Hannah — with her bare hands.

At one spot on the road to Zmerinka, an oily black cloud ascended from behind a hill. One of Hannah's companions shouted, "The Gaidamaks are burning the houses in the outskirts of the city." Hannah galloped to the rear of her squadron, where several hundreds Red cavalrymen were resting around a small pond. The men were lying about talking with each other, playing cards, and smoking. Hannah shouted a command to mount their horses and join her soldiers in a frontal attack against the insurgents in the burning settlements. "The smoke will shield us from their gun fire. We will surround them and teach them a lesson!" In an hour the Reds surrounded the entire insurgent force. Thunder of canon was heard along the battle field. The insurgents, blinded by the heavy smoke, expecting no attack from the rear, could not repell the sudden assault. Those who did not perish from the gun fire surrendered. Hannah, though happy at the decisive victory over the enemy, nontheless shed tears at the corpses devoured by fire and sword. Unfortunately, this was her last exploit.

One cloudy day the pogromist troops of Sokolov attacked Hannah's brigade and she was taken prisoner. The guards taking her to their commander's headquarters were armed with rifles, pistols, and sabres. One of them carried a light machine gun on his back. They stopped to rest in a small pine grove. It began to rain, and the heavy drops wiped out every other sound. The darkness was so dense that one could not distinguish a man from a bush. Suddenly shots were heard. The guards spread out and crawled on their stomachs. Shots rang out again from all sides. They heard horses galloping. Hannah grabbed the gun of the soldier nearest her and tripped him. When he fell, she smashed his head with the rifle butt. Two riders, Hannah's two sons, dismounted, and the three hurled themselves on the three remaining guards. The guards were quickly disarmed. Hannah removed three knives from their belts and hid them in her bosom. She and her sons found shelter in a fortified hut, which served the local peasants and travellers as a hostel. The mother talked to her sons in whispers. She told them the story of another Hannah, who, in ancient times, sacrificed her seven sons rather than be humiliated by the enemy of their people. She related stories of Jewish anguish and martyrdom, the current pogroms, the killing of their grandfather, and beseeched them to choose death by their own hand rather than fall into the hands of the vicious hooligans, the Jew killers. She also recited to her sons a section of Bialik's* poem "The City of Slaughter", which is both a protest against the bestiality of the massacre in Kishineff in 1903 and an expression of rage against the helplessness of the victims. The poem begins with the words, "Of steel and iron, cold and hard and dumb, Now forge thyself a heart, O Man, and come and walk the town of slaughter".

"Have a heart of stone, my sons," she said, "Die without fear."

Before dawn search parties of Gaidamacks were sent out to find the fugitives. They were found and an exchange of fire ensued. When Hannah and her sons ran out of ammunition they engaged in hand to hand fighting — the three against the eight. When Hannah saw the odds against them, she offered to surrender on condition that the savage fighting stop.

A lone lantern lit up the murky dawn. The soldiers marched in two columns behind Hannah and her sons. Their faces were covered with coagulated blood, their clothes were in tatters. When they approached the Gaidamack headquarters they saw three gallows prepared for them. The sons pulled out their mouth organs and began to play the Hasidic chant: "And take Your people out of exile". The tune was so enchanting and so sorrowful that even the cold-blooded killers stood aghast. As the tune flowed from the lips of her sons, Hannah raised her eyes to heaven, as if in prayer to the One who dwells on high. When the playing came to an end, Hannah thrust two sharp knives straight into the chests of her brave sons. They fell dead at her feet. Her face was contorted by the excruciating spasm of pain as she plunged the third knife into her own heart. "It is better to die by one's own hand than to be killed by these butchers! Long live the Jewish people!" she shouted, and fell dead.

The commander who had come to oversee the hanging sighed. The soldiers made the sign of the cross. A few knelt in prayer. In the diary of one of them was inscribed the following eulogy: "I shall never forget the face of this heroic mother and proud soldier."

Isaiah Bunis

To the left of Grandfather's home was Isaiah's textile goods store, a shop justly renowned for its orderliness, cleanliness and embellishments. The bolts of cotton and linen were arranged on the lower shelves; woolens, covered for protection against moths by white sheets, were on the middle shelves; while the colorful silks, satins and velvets were resplendent on the top shelves. On weekdays, early in the morning, Isaiah would rise to sweep and polish the floor of the store, dust the counters, arrange the displays of piecegoods to attract the eyes of the customers, wipe the haze from the show window, and lastly, retreat to the desk in the back of the store to write down the orders for Berl the Buyer, who did the purchasing for all the shopkeepers in town in the wholesale houses of the city of Berditchev.

When these chores were finished Isaiah would go outside for a bit of fresh air. This apparently pleased him so much that he would often burst out laughing out of sheer good spirits. People were greatly amazed by the sight of a man standing alone in the street laughing out loud. When asked why this sudden jollity, he would say: "When I observe my neighboring storekeepers holed up in their stores, these bent, anemic sad people, worn down by endless hours of waiting for a customer, I cannot help laughing. My competitors don't know how to deal with the peasants, nor are they proficient in Ukrainian dialects; their accented speech arouses the contempt of the gentiles and their behavior frequently annoys every red blooded peasant."

And truth to tell, Isaiah was the most successful salesman of textiles on the entire block; for the peasants, after rummaging in the stores of several of Isaiah's competitors, came back to him where they were served promptly and satisfactorily. They listened to his expert advice as to the value and price of various fabrics, interlaced with jokes, epigrams and compliments; they bargained a bit — as is customary — and in the end bought what he had recommended in the first place. He seemed to have a hypnotic power over them. Men and women, old and young, were flattered by his admiration of their youthful healthy appearance, delivered in honey-sweet words, which paved the way for expenditures which benefited both the buyer and the seller simultaneously.

But his intimates knew that there was another reason for his laughter. He laughed because he, who was born and raised in the dense forest of Priluki, whose youthful years were spent among the peasantry in the country, should end up as a pitiful petty merchant. Who would have thought that the "prankster", as he was called in his childhood, would be tamed and "caught in the trap" of trading and bartering for a living in this miserable little town, where even the air for breathing was foul and scarce. He laughed at the irony of fate which incarcerated a free spirit like his in the narrow confines of a small store, like all those petty Jewish storekeepers who waste their lives away in the malodorous cubicles of the market place. Who could have imagined for one moment that Isaiah, who was the boon companion of men of muscle and brawn, who lived close to "mother nature" and whose wives, sons and daughters were as stout and solid as the trees of the forest, would be forced to spend the rest of his days in the company of peddlers and hawkers of novelties and notions, of pins and needles — toothless gnomes and crones who didn't have the strength to draw water from the well or split wood from the forest.

How then did Isaiah get stuck in town as a storekeeper? When his father died, he was only sixteen years old. His mother struggled to make a living for the family, which included two grown, marriagable daughters. Without the guiding hand of a father, Isaiah grew up wild in the country. So the widow sold the property which she inherited from her husband and moved to town, where she opened a drygoods store. But even the store did not bring in enough to support the household. So she sent her handsome son to the fairs to sell all kinds of trinkets that women fancy: combs, ribbons, cosmetics, needles and threads, ointments, semi-precious stones and beads, and religious articles. Isaiah attracted the admiring glances of the peasant women with his handsome virility, and made many a conquest and many a sale. When his mother died, in his twentieth year, he met at one of the fairs a girl of our town, the tall and pretty Leah. He fell in love with her, and after an arduous courtship they were married. With the dowry they built a house, the largest room of which was fixed up as a fabric shop. Isaiah was so deeply in love with his young wife that he was willing to do whatever she asked of him, even to become a storekeeper. And wondrous to behold — the store became a challenge to him! He made every effort to acquire the merchandise which the customers wanted, to keep the shop neat and clean, and to receive all comers with a lively and pleasant disposition.

After a while Isaiah began to feel stifled in the store and restless at home. He was intensely envious of the peasants who were free to roam the fields and woods. That is when he developed the nervous habit of laughing hysterically. It was as if he were expressing contempt for his predicament in being confined to the restricted circle of his life and occupation when his soul yearned to cleave to nature, to lose himself in the tall corn and the thick pine groves of the great outdoors. In the quiet of the night, when his vital forces strained to break out from the inhibitions of conventional morality, Isaiah would leave the house to roam the villages seeking amatory adventures. When Leah discovered that her husband was running after young peasant women, she swallowed her pride and hid her sorrow. When she became pregnant and felt the sweet anticipation of approaching motherhood, she bore her suffering over her husband's faithlessness in silence. She bore a son, who was named after her late father, Menachem. Leah anxiously cared for the infant, who was her only solace in her grief.

Years passed. The son grew up to become an outstanding scholar, intelligent and hardworking. Isaiah hired two private tutors for him, one for Talmud and another for secular subjects. Both testified that the boy was a genius. Leah willingly accepted her husband's suggestion to send the boy to study in the Gymanasium (secondary school) in the city of Lipovitz.

The mother was now lonelier than ever, even though Isaiah made every effort to treat her with tenderness and to show her signs of affection. She cried a great deal, kept to the house, and ventured out only on market days to help her husband in the business. Otherwise, she walked about the house silent and sorrowful, and practiced sexual abstinence from her husband by making his bed in the store. Without too much investigation Leah knew of her husband's infidelity, yet she continued to love him.

One rainy night, when Isaiah failed to come home, Leah went out to look for him. She went straight to the yards of the peasant huts, and in one of them heard her husband's loud laughter emanating from the barn. She returned home wet from the rain and shivering from excitement. From that night on there was a distinct change in her appearance. Her palor, the lack of luster in her eyes, her poor posture and her obvious lack of energy indicated that she was seriously ill. After a while she began to develop a chronic cough. The town physician, Dr. Tshikovsky, was a frequent visitor in her house. Yet, although Isaiah worried greatly over his wife's illness and spent much time at her bedside, there was little change in his way of life. When the spirit of mischief befell him, he disappeared for days to carouse in the company of his gentile companions.

When his son became 15 years old, and was a matriculated student of the fifth grade in the Gymnasium, Isaiah was hastily called to the hospital of Lipovitz, where his son was ill with tuberculosis. The doctors advised that he be taken at once to a well known sanitarium in Austria. There, high in the mountains, among the vineyards, he would recover his health. When Isaiah saw his son lying in bed with his face to the wall, a shiver ran down his spine. With tears in his eyes he sat down at the side of the bed and for a long while silently observed his sick only son.

A few days later Isaiah and his son traveled to the T.B. sanitarium in Austria. On the way he got to know his son's problems, not only his deteriorating health and the lack of harmony between his parents, but the antagonistic attitude toward him as a Jew on the part of the students and teachers in his school. He seemed particularly disturbed by the virulent anti-Semitism of the academic community. He described for his father the expression of utter contempt on the face of the teacher of Russian literature, which seemed to say: "What is this little 'Zhid' (a humiliating name for Jews) doing in the Gymanasium? He was aware of the current ideals of progress and liberalism which prevailed among educated people, but was saddened by the fact that those ideals somehow excluded a change of attitude toward the Jewish group. Even the socialists maintained that the Jews were exploiters of the people, leaches, who sucked the blood of the peasantry, let alone the reactionary elements who considered the Jews as the leaders of rebellion, who aroused the masses to revolt against the Fatherland and its Tzarist regime.

When Isaiah heard his son's report of his experiences in the non-Jewish environment and his explanation of the nature of Jewish economy, he realized that he had been unjust in condemning the Jews for leading unproductive lives in petty trade, while he admired the gentiles as sturdy tillers of the soil who earned their daily bread "by the sweat of their brow". He recalled those very same Jews on their Sabbaths and festivals giving off an air of spiritual mobility, as if truly accompanied by the "Ministering Angels".

Soon Menachem settled in the sanitarium and his father hurried back home. Isaiah realized that he must undergo a change of heart and behavior for the sake of his sick wife and son. When he arrived home, it suddenly occurred to him to sell all the merchandise in the store, give up his business and bring his wife to the same sanitarium in Austria. In the presence of her son she was apt to get a new lease on life. He talked the matter over with Leah, who was astounded at the change in her husband's outlook toward their life.

It took about a month to liquidate the business. What was left of the stock, after four consecutive market days, was sold to another store keeper for a pittance. They locked up the house and left town in a hurry. When Isaiah was alone with his wife in the train compartment, she seemed as beautiful to him as in the days of their courtship. He decided then and there to make up to her for the past seventeen years of suffering and humiliation. She finally faced him with the challenging question: "Do you really intend to give up your pursuit of the 'shikses' (gentile girls)?" Whereupon he embraced her and kissed her and cuddled her in his arms until she fell asleep.

Many months passed, during which Leah and her son gradually recovered in the sanitarium. Isaiah never failed to pay the bills, nor to keep them informed and happy with his long affectionate letters. Once in three months he would visit them bearing gifts. He would never discuss his business affairs, as if it did not concern them. They only knew that he lived in the city of Uman, but did not know that he also traveled far and wide to many fairs. He never told them, for instance, that for a period of nine months he was engaged in horse trading, in partnership with two young peasants. Once he suspected them of stealing one of the horses and selling it to one of his competitors. He lost his temper and attacked them. In the ensuing bout both sides gave as well as they got. Isaiah barely escaped with his life, left the horse trading business, and got himself a job in one of the feed warehouses of Uman.

The Jewish population of Uman was nearly forty thousand. Isaiah became friendly with the brother of his employer, an erudite Jew, who had mastered the Russian language. On his recommendation Isaiah joined the evening course for adults at the Zionist community center. He devoted himself to the study of Jewish history, Bible and Hebrew literature, and made considerable strides in those subjects. One of the teachers gave him private instruction in Russian and mathematics. Isaiah became so self-confident that he undertook to deliver a lecture on the value of agriculture in the resettlement of Palestine.

When he visited his wife and son in the sanitarium for the last time his manner was that of a "scholar and gentleman": He spoke Yiddish impeccably, he seemed to be very relaxed and self-assured as a genuine citizen of the world. The wife and the boy were overjoyed when he suggested that they join him in his apartment in Uman. But on the train home they learned of the outbreak of war. Isaiah greeted this terrible news with his old nervous reaction of loud laughter. He stood in the middle of the railroad car and laughed uncontrollably. Leah was shocked, for she recognized the symptoms of the old character blemish of her husband — hysteria in the face of sudden adversity. This sudden shock brought on a paroxysm of coughing, which turned the joyous journey into a nightmare. Worried and tense, they arrived in our town to their old house, which had been desolate for two years.

When the son was called to the army, and was exempted from military service, after an exhaustive physical examination by the army doctors, Isaiah was in the town of Geissin working in an arms manufacturing plant. As an essential worker in a defense plant, he, too, was deferred from the draft. He wrote home long letters explaining his desire to leave Russia and settle in Palestine. His plan was to send the son to Odessa to investigate the possibility of finding a ship which would cross the Black Sea on its way to Istanbul. There was a substantial Jewish community in the Turkish capital, and he could live among them until he found a ship bound for Palestine. He suggested that on the way to Odessa the son stop in Geissin to get the necessary funds and to take leave of his father.

But the plan did not materialize. For lack of proper nutrition, and from too much anxiety, the son became ill again. When Isaiah heard of it, he sought ways of quitting his job in the plant in order to return home. At last, he employed the desperate device of having two of his fingers caught and cut off in the bayonet sharpening machine. He was allowed to leave and returned home before his hand had healed.

As soon as he opened the door of his house he began to laugh. As he proceeded further into the house, and upon crossing the threshold into his son's bedroom, his laugh became hysterical. Leah fell back on an old remedy. She asked the boy to sing a gypsy song which seemed to settle his father's nerves. Menachem sang with spirit, the father listened attentively, and an atmosphere of unselfish love enveloped the sickroom.

Little by little, life returned to normal. The boy's health improved somewhat. Isaiah and Leah frequented the fairs and eeked out a livelihood. The doctor kept up his medicating routine and the reliable Hannah-Rivah supplied them with sweet cream and eggs and other rich foods ordered by the physician. Peace seemed at last to have descended on Isaiah's homestead.

Then the whole Ukraine was weighted down by a smog of black clouds as the hurrican of revolution swept over Russia. In the dark of night, shrieks of terror and wails of lamentation rent the still air, as bloodthirsty bands of murderers roamed and ravaged the Jewish towns, killing, raping and looting. The civil war brought about violent clashes between the Soviet government and the insurgent bands of Ukrainian nationalists. These clashes assumed a specially dangerous scope for the Jewish communities. The motto of the Gaidamacks "Kill the Jewish rabble! Save the Ukraine!"

aroused the uncouth and uneducated masses, who joined the bands of hooligans and reduced many a Jewish community to ashes.

On the tenth of Tammuz, in the year 1919, when the pogrom hit our town, Leah and her son, Menachem, found shelter in a special hiding place in the cellar of their home; Isaiah refused to hide. He walked swiftly to the home of his Christian friends to solicit their help in preventing bloodshed. While Isaiah was away from his house, two of the marauders found the entrance to this refuge, which was hidden under a rug. The cellar, half of which was occupied by blocks of ice covered by rags to keep them from melting quickly, and half by mounds of potatoes and barrels of preserved fruit and vegetables, aroused the curiousity of the bandits, who decided to make a thorough search for concealed valuables. In their rummaging they discovered the two refugees and began to beat them. One of them was about to lower his sabre on Menachem's head, when Isaiah suddenly appeared on the scene, tore the sabre from the hand of the bandit and waiving it wildly, wounded the attackers severely. When they came up from the cellar into the kitchen they were met by two drunken Gaida-macks, who were carrying sacks full of loot. Isaiah began to laugh, which made the bandits think he was trying to amuse them, so they ordered him to sing and dance for them. Isaiah communicated to Leah in a singsong to remove from her bosom the little bundle of paper money which she had hidden there. Leah did as he told her, and when the bandits fell upon her to grab the money, Isaiah kicked them with all his remaining strength. They fell on the floor dripping blood. Isaiah with his wife and son managed to escape to the house of the friendly priest, who saved the lives of many other Jews.

Menachem's health deteriorated, yet he wished to join other young men who were being recruited for the Jewish self-defense units. But the doctor would not hear of it. Isaiah held long conversations with his son, deploring the fact that Jews were hiding in holes and able-bodied men were crawling into burrows instead of offering resistance to the rioting mobs. He berated himself, a man known in the past for his bravery and prowess, for following the cowardly example of the others, instead of trampling the verminous vipers into the dust. Where was our pride, our honor? Is it only in Palestine that our youth dare to stand up against attack? Why not here, also, meet force with force, and die defending life and property, if necessary, and never bend the head before every thief and murderer! Isaiah did not realize that with such harangues he was causing his son to disregard the doctor's order and to volunteer for the self-defense forces. Indeed, one day Menachem left the house. His father looked for him in the nearby towns and villages. He found his body by the roadside leading toward Priluki beside three other defenders who fought back. When he returned home his laughing spells could not be stopped by his desperate and disconsolate wife.

That very night a self-defense brigade was organized in our town, consisting of a few men armed with pistols and rifles led by Isaiah. The next few days others joined the group. By the end of the week the number of armed men reached 39. One night in the month of Elul a troop of bandits surrounded Isaiah and his fellow fighters. The insurgents wanted to find out the identity of the Bolshevik commissars in the town. Isaiah insisted that there were no commissars there, and when asked: "Who are you, then?" He proudly replied: "We are the guardians of the community!" Fortunately, the bandits were in a hurry to rally to their commander in Zazov; otherwise, Isaiah and his little army would have been involved in a desperate and uneven battle.

On the fourth day of the Intermediate Days of the festival of Succoth,* disorganized Bolshevik troops retreating from their defeat in Poland reached our town. In the distillery they found barrels of whisky. They got themselves thoroughly drunk and took out their frustrations on the Jewish homes during six consecutive days of unmitigated horror. They burned down scores of houses, brutally killed dozens of people, looted stores and warehouses, and roamed the streets howling their ribald marching songs. In Isaiah's house they raped his wife in front of his eyes and tortured him cruelly. On the third day of the pogrom Isaiah got a hold of a horse and galloped to Vinnitza, where a whole brigade of the Red Army was stationed. After convincing the commander of the brigade that the criminals in our town were renegade Red Army soldiers, he was assured by the commander that the culprits would be severely punished. At the head of a cavalry troop was Isaiah leading the way, the Reds surrounded the town, captured and disarmed the renegades, and those who offered resistance to arrest were shot on the spot. Isaiah recognized the man who had raped his wife and avenged his wife's dishonor by killing him. When the commander found out about it he reprimanded him for taking the law into his own hands. But Isaiah ignored his warning and spent many hours looking for the soldier who had despoiled his home. His wife begged him not to spill any more blood, but he reacted to her pleas with laughter. When he raised a sword over the head of one of the suspects, a shot was heard. Isaiah fell gravely wounded. The commander returned his pistol to the holster and left the house. Isaiah breathed his last in his wife's arms. For the last time he laughed, this time weakly, as he always did in critical moments.

Yavdokha

A young, full-bodied woman of average height, broad, high forehead, and heavy auburn hair, plaited in two thick braids at the nape of her neck, her full lips quivering sensously, revealing brightly shining teeth, her blue eyes smiling reflecting strength and energy — and her whole body radiating a self-confident femininity — that was the peasant woman Yavdokha.

The small modest house she lived in stood near the Christian cemetery, hidden in a small grove of trees, out of sight of passers by. Her husband Yefim, a diligent worker, was the keeper of the cemetery; he had many tasks: supervision of the two grave diggers, guarding the wreaths of flowers on the graves, clearing the paths between the rows of graves in the wintertime, cultivating the shrubs and flowerbeds in the spring and in the summer. In all these jobs Yavdokha was his reliable assistant, just as she was his true helpmate at home, growing vegetables in the garden, running the spinning wheel in the house, mending garments and hosiery, and doing all the housework — cooking, cleaning and washing.

Yavdokha often came to the Jewish stores to buy candles, ribbons, spices — all according to her husband's instructions. From time to time she visited old Breina seeking a cure for barrenness, for she yearned to be a mother. When Breina, playing with her two year old grandchild, would hand him over to Yavdokha, a delicious feeling of sweetness and warmth came over her. She would cuddle the small warm body in her arms and think to herself: "How good it is to be a mother. . ."

Her husband Yefim loved her passionately and believed that they were denied offspring as a retribution for his youthful indiscretion. That is why he drank moderately, did not scold his wife, and never squandered his money. In the winter, when the mysterious stillness of the long nights engulfed their hearts, souls, and bodies, they sang melancholy songs or read aloud to one another. In the summer they spent every free hour working in the garden or puttering around the house.

When World War I broke out, her husband was drafted into the army and sent to the front. Soon after, Yavdokha received sad news that Yefim had been killed in battle with the Germans. Now a war widow, she was overcome with grief and worries. Since the house was church property and went with the job of tending the cemetery, she kept the news of her husband's death from the priest. She was afraid she would be evicted from the house. Eventually, she had to go to the clergyman, who could not help being aroused by the sight of her voluptous body and pretty face — there was that certain something in the woman that could turn the head of any vigorous male. But the priest was a good and right-thinking individual, and he restrained his passion. He offered her fatherly advice and allowed her to keep her house on condition that she carry out her husband's duties fully. Yavdokha performed her tasks conscientiously and resumed her visits to town.

In her youth Yavdokha had worked every Friday in the home of a well-to-do Jew who lived in Kalinovka, about two miles from her native village. This man treated her kindly and respectfully, not like a maid but more like a guest who helped with the housework. He encouraged her to study, gave her books, and frequently explained difficult texts. The lady of the house, a thin sickly woman who frequently coughed until sweat covered her forehead from the exertion, also treated her kindly and spoke lovingly to her. They were an unusual couple; young Yavdokha loved them. When she had to leave her village after her wedding, she shed tears over having to part from these Jewish "saints". In Vakhnovka, where she settled with her husband, she avoided mentioning the couple in conversation, because Yefim hated Jews and spoke ill of them. He also restricted her visits to Jewish homes to business dealings. Old Breina, who reminded her of her former mistress in Kalinovka, she saw more often, and came to love her dearly.

After the death of her husband, the priest had convinced her that it was sinful to hate fellow human beings, for all men were created in God's image, and Jews were human, too. Yavdokha began to feel more at ease with her Jewish friends, and her visits to their homes were more frequent. She was especially fond of visiting the Moreinis home, where she met young, intelligent people, who spoke Russian well and treated her as a sincere friend. There she also borrowed books, which in spite of their difficult vocabulary, gave her great satisfaction. Although she craved the company of a man and yearned for sexual fulfillment, she waited patiently for one she could really love.

One evening early in spring, when the trees had barely begun to bud, a group of these elegant young people met in her house. She had cleaned thoroughly, and her home sparkled with cheerfulness and festivity. The meeting was such a success that from then on the group met often in Yavdokha's garden, or when it rained, in her little house. Yavdokha learned a great deal from them about the oppressive Tzarist regime and their dreams of social liberation. She recovered completely from her depression over her husband's death, finding consolation in the books and in the lively conversations of her friends. When she sang Ukrainian folksongs to entertain her guests, she seemed like a wilted tree that had suddenly burst into bloom. Gradually, she developed an emotional attachment to a young student who spent many hours in her house, and whose intimate serenading filled her heart with tremulous joy. In his close presence she was overpowered by a desire that demanded consummation. Later, when he left town, she was consoled by intimate relations with another young man, and later, with still another . . . When winter came and young men, most of them students, left town, her house became the center of entertainment for the local intelligentsia, including some middle-aged men.

Among those who knew Yavdokha well, stories circulated that on winter nights when the white snow covered the ground, the wind ran wild in the fields, and no living soul was to be seen, Yavdokha would banish the loneliness that pervaded her house by inviting one of her acquaintances in and asking him to take the clear night air with her. And when the two of them went out together, they would fling themselves to the ground and roll in the snow with childish glee. Yavdokha would screech and laugh, burning with excitement, but suddenly she would jump up and run away. If her friend could not catch up and overtake her, the peasant girl would disappear behind a mound of snow. There she would wait while the young man called and searched for her, until he would finally lose patience and angrily go home. Not so with the man who pursued and found her. They would return to her room, where with a radiant face Yavdokha would delight her guest with warm caresses and embraces. There were rumors that once a rich man came to see her, and she chased him away because he offered her money and dared to approach her. Yavdovkha had no desire for money, nor did she accept gifts. She did not allow the rich townspeople to cross her threshold, but bestowed her favors only on those who attracted her through their masculinity, their pleasantness of manner, their fine qualities, their simplicity and originality in both thought and deed. That is why she was nicknamed *tshestnaya davalka,* "the one who offers herself out of an honest feeling of love."

A few months after her husband's death Yavdokha had gone once more to Breina to ask for advice regarding conception. The old woman shook her head and said that widows have no need for such potions, but Yavdokha smiled and answered: "If my womb opens, the child will be conceived by the Holy Ghost. It has happened before, you know. . ." This was what the wise old woman secretly reported to her friend Chana Leah. Both of them, it seemed, wished Yavdokha well.

In the meantime the war ended, and the turmoil that followed in the wake of the revolution caused great restlessness. The Tzar was deposed, the people took the reins of state in hand. Hooligan factions and troops of the Ukrainian Republic Army, headed by the Ataman S.V. Petlura, spread throughout the Ukraine. The civil war between the "Reds" and the "Whites" reached its zenith. Bands of soldiers from both camps conquered communities in quick succession looting, burning, and killing. Gaidamack* calvary units broke into defenseless towns and villages and terrorized their inhabitants with fire and sword.

In the summer of 1919 the holocaust reached most of the Jewish communities of the Ukraine. In many places self-defense units were organized. In other places combined committees of Jews and Gentiles were established to approach the commanders of the rioting military units with petitions and bribes of appeasement. In some towns the self-defense groups fought back bravely, communicating regularly with the Soviet forces, which were generally concentrated around the railroad stations. Many engagements were fought by the Ukrainian partisans and the Soviet militia, in whose ranks were many Jews. The Soviet militia, small but well-disciplined and highly motivated forces, would attack the enemy from the rear, thus saving some Jewish communities from a direct frontal attack.

Yavdokha was emotionally attached to the countryside, but felt badly about the events of the period. She was torn between a great love for the Ukrainian people, which was throwing off the yoke of the century-long Tzarist oppression, and her affection for the Jews, among whom she had found friendship and spiritual fulfillment. Unconsciously, she veered toward the latter, meeting frequently with Jewish leaders, to whom she passed valuable information about the intentions and plans of the peasants in the neighboring villages. Yavdokha kept them well informed of the ever increasing danger.

A few days before the arrival of Tutiuniuk's force to our town, Vakhnovka, Yavdokha came, greatly excited, to the home of Moreinis to tell about the pogroms in Somegorodok, a Jewish community about 25 miles away. She suggested that we begin at once laying away groceries and currency to bribe the commander of the troops. Insisting that the peasantry favored the Jews of the town, she advised that we ask their support for the Jewish leaders when they go out to ask the Ukrainian bands not to loot and kill. She volunteered to intercede with Tutuniuk's adjutant, a former resident of her village, and try to convince him that the Jews were decent people — not a communist among them! She hinted that if words would not be sufficient to achieve her goal, she was prepared to employ other means. Furthermore, we had to have the full cooperation of the priest, and see that he would do whatever he could.

Everything was done as Yavdokha suggested. When the bandits arrived at the outskirts of town — horsemen and infantry, with wagonloads of loot, the members of the town committee accompanied by the peasant leaders went out to meet Tutiuniuk, commander of the band.

But Tutiunik did not restrain his men from robbing and killing wantonly and cruelly. Yavdokha was cleaning her room after the departure of her former townsman, the adjutant of Tutiuniuk, who had promised to influence his chief to restrain the troops, when she heard shooting and screams of victims. She realized that after the officers left their troops, even if they had warned them to keep peace, the bloodthirsty killers had not been able to control themselves. She rushed to the center of town, and was aghast at what she saw there. She ran to the priest's house, her hair disheveled, and would not leave until he put on his clerical robe and accompanied her. All day they ran from place to place, helping victims, doing whatever they could. Towards evening, after the bandits departed, and people began emerging from their hiding places to look for relatives, Yavdokha started home along the street that led to the cemetery.

Approaching the Christian cemetery, she saw a group of women standing in a circle looking at the ground. She peered through the circle and saw three corpses, apparently the bodies of Jews who had been dragged there from town and tortured to death. With a heart-rending cry she prostrated herself over the bodies and burst into tears. The women, most of them quite young, looked with amazement at the Gentile woman grieving over the dead Jews. One of them, bending down to raise Yavdokha, grabbed the "peculiar" organ, and waved it in the air to the derision and delight of her friends: "Look at the virility of this 'zhid'* — how funny it looks!" One by one the women examined the limp member and kneaded it, as if they were pulling on the teats of a cow's udder, all the while laughing hysterically. Yavdokha picked up a stray board, and shouting curses at her vile sisters for profaning the body of a martyr, she rained heavy blows on their heads.

The women ran away. Yavdokha took off her shawl and covered the lower parts of the naked bodies. When the families of the murdered men arrived, she helped them load the bodies on a wagon, and accompanied them back to town.

A week later we learned that in the nearby town of Priluki, the troops of the partisan chieftain Sokolov, a loose band of cut-throats from various military units of Petlura's forces, had perpetrated a horrible massacre. We realized how close we were to the same fate. Sokolov was infamous as a merciless butcher. A meeting was called and it was hastily decided to evacuate the population to the city of Lipovitz, 18 miles away, where a number of Red Army units were stationed. In no time a large crowd gathered in the marketplace — men, women, and children carrying treasured possessions — ready to leave. The peasants of the town's outskirts were pleading with them to remain and weather the storm. Yavdokha, too, begged them not to endanger the lives of so many people by exposing them to the perils of the open road. She ran from one group of frightened people to another and tried to reassure them. The priest also urged the people to stay, promising to protect them with his very life, if necessary. But the Jews were convinced that even with the best intentions of these friendly Gentiles, they could not stand up to Sokolov and his cohorts. With the help of the elder of the peasants, a good friend of hers, Yavdokha mobilized about twenty other peasants to transport the women, children, and sick in their wagons. Yavdokha also organized another group of peasants to stand guard at the houses of the evacuees. Eight days later when the refugees returned home, they found everything in place — nothing was missing.

One night at the end of the month of Tammuz (corresponding to the month of July), Tutiuniuk returned. His adjutant went to Yavdokha's home raging: Why did she, a faithful and devout Christian, post guards around the Jewish town to defend those Communist Christ-killers? Her argument that Jews were also human beings, that one God had created us all, Jews and Christians alike, fell on deaf ears. The officer ridiculed her maudlin soft-heartedness, recounting his adventures in the province: how many houses he had set on fire, how many Jewish women he had raped, how many he had murdered. Yavdokha looked at him with disgust. When he bent down to embrace her, a wave of nausea rose in her throat and a shudder of fear crept over her body. She extricated herself from his arms and retreated toward the door. When he reached for her, and she stepped back through the open door, he tripped and fell on his face; his injured nose bled. She grabbed a broom and beat him heftily. Then she ran from the place and hid among the tallest of the gravestones in the cemetery. Late that night, she saw columns of smoke rising from the direction of the marketplace and sparks that scorched the kindled flames in the trees of her grove — the officer had put her house on fire as punishment for the beating she had given him. The realization made her jump, as if bitten by a snake, and she ran for the priest's house. She heard shots and windows shattering. A few Jews, running into the priest's yard for shelter, told her that one of the officers was running riot in the streets, shouting: "Death to all Jews! Death to Jew lovers!" Having no roof over her head in Vakhnovka and all her goods having gone up in smoke, Yavdokha went to live in Kalinovka, the town close to her birthplace. There, with the help of her Jewish and Gentile friends, she organized a civil guard from among the town's youth. In one confrontation between a Soviet military unit allied with the local militia and a partisan band of Petlura, Yavdokha recognized among the latter the officer who had burned down her house. She shouted in an inhuman voice: "Murderer!" The officer turned toward her, two shots were heard, and both fell to the ground. The officer died instantly of a bullet in his brain; Yovdokha was badly wounded in the shoulder and was taken to a hospital.

While recuperating in the hospital she gave a good deal of thought to the lot of her people, the oppressed peasantry, and to the suffering of the Jews. She was sympathetic to the down-trodden masses of both peoples. She was convinced that the poor peasants could not be helped by the Ukrainian nationalists, nor could the Jews expect a better life under their regime. That is why she decided to join the Red Army. The Communists, she reasoned, are honest men, ready to sacrifice their lives for justice and equality. Their victory will also be the victory of all oppressed nationalities.

In the hospital she met Joseph, a young man who had been wounded in a battle with Petlura's forces. He sang and played the mandolin expertly, like a professional folk singer. She was greatly agitated by the sad overtones of his melodies, which often moved her to tears. After her discharge from the hospital, she joined the Red Army unit stationed in Kalinovka, but returned to visit him. His bodily wounds healed slowly, but his mental wound remained very painful. Yavdokha understood that his was the suffering of a man yearning for salvation for himself and the world. Once she found him sitting on his bed, his head covered, chanting a song soul-shattering in its poignant beauty. When he finished, he told her that it was a Jewish prayer called "Kol Nidre," a declaration of faith and a supplication for forgiveness, which ushers in the most solemn Jewish festival — Yom Kippur. From that day she questioned him more and more about Jewish customs and rituals. She discovered that he was shocked and spiritually shattered by the horror of the pogroms. He seemed to echo the bewilderment of the biblical Gideon, who asked: "If God is with us, why has all this happened to us?" He spoke tensely about man's eternal quest for redemption and for a better social order. Yavdokha experienced anguish as she never had before when she listened to this young Jew.

She began to feel her Communist faith melting away when confronted with his relentless description and stark analysis of social reality. She ceased to believe in the "best of all possible worlds" in the presence of this amazing young Jew, and worried lest she fall into the abyss of disillusionment that he seemed to open before her. Yet, she wanted to share his sorrow and suffering.

At the end of the Jewish month of Kislev on the third night of the festival of Hanukkah, they met on the banks of the river Dniester, not far from the little town of Sgoritza, on the Russian-Rumanian border. They had decided to escape from blood-soaked Russia. If they could cross the border without arousing the suspicion of the border guards on both sides, they would happily start a new life. . .

Yavdokha knew that she was being hunted as a deserter from the Red Army, and if caught, she would be shot. Her Jewish suitor was baffled: "Was she really ready to abandon her Christian upbringing and her recent conversion to Communism? Would she exchange them for the nebulous vision of a prophetic apocatypse as embodied in the brotherly commune of a kibbutz in the Galilee?"

****

I met this couple in the agricultural colony Messilah Hadashah ("The New Road"), established by ICA* near Istanbul, Turkey, in 1921 during the intermediate days of Passover. Yavdokha and her young husband, the "Strange Jew", who had joined the third commune of HeHalutz*, were training in the colony. They both worked in the fields during the morning hours, studied Hebrew in the afternoons, and participated in heated discussions on the functions of HeHalutz in the evenings. One evening, following a visit by the poet Saul Tchernichowsky, the discussion centered on the renewed pogroms in the Ukraine. Yavdokha ascended the rock at the gate of the settlement, which served as a platform for speakers and discussion leaders, and recited in Russian translation Tchernichowsky's poem, "This Be Our Revenge". The poet himself had read the poem in Hebrew a few days earlier at a reception in Istanbul and Yavdokha's husband had translated it into Russian. It reads as follows:*

THIS WILL BE OUR REVENGE

We shall not go up against you,
As you do; nor shall we set fire
To your roofs over your heads, and with iron bars
We shall not shatter the skulls of babes!
Not until with your strong hand you have uprooted,
Not until your contaminated palms have erased altogether
The image of God stamped upon us,
The tokens of ancient nobility of spirit,
And of descent from princely generations —
All we have gathered, all we have delivered into the hearts of men,

Little by little, in gleams and sparks,
Through hundreds of jubilees and hundreds of generations,
Which we have reared in asceticism and chastity
And the yoke of the Ten Commandments.

Yavdokha the "giyoret" ("convert to Judaism") and her husband, the regenerated Jew, became the favorites of the whole group. Every evening they sang and danced exuberantly with their comrades, intoxicated with their new faith. Joseph would play the mandolin, accompanying Yavdokha's deep contralto voice. When the two of them sang, their beaming faces reflecting an inner radiance, it seemed as if heavenly bliss had descended upon this community of young men and women, who dreamed of a new life in Palestine and the universal salvation of mankind.

Grandfather

My Grandfather was a very busy and serious man. When I recall him, I see him in five distinct situations.

I see him in the darkness of winter nights, walking energetically toward his goal through the empty streets, bundled up in his heavy overcoat. He strides firmly forward, his trousers stuck in his boots, his hat tied with a kerchief tucked under his chin, carrying a lantern in his gloved hand and breathing heavily against the biting wind. From the windows stare small lights which stab into the darkness of the night. He listens to the sounds of the deep night with his head raised on high, and his footsteps on the frozen snow make a rhythmic series of groans and squeaks.

I see him again on a market day as he stands in his store. He leans against the southern wall near the door holding a copy of the Midrash Rabba*, in which he reviews the biblical portion of the week. When a customer enters, he puts the book away in a drawer and, if the caller is a man, puts out his hand in greeting, or sets out a chair if the caller is a woman. He converses with them in Ukrainian mixed with Polish idioms. He always tries to create an atmosphere of relaxation and friendship, as if he were thinking: This is the will of the Creator — that a man should be sociable and friendly with all people.

On the Sabbath I see him in a corner of the synagogue reading the portion of the week from an open Torah scroll on an elevated desk. The poor people of the town are seldom called to the reading of the Torah at the central pulpit, but here in Grandfather's corner they are important and feel a sense of self-worth. For Grandfather calls them not merely for an Aliyah* to intone the prescribed blessing, but bestows upon them the honor of "Shelishi"* or even "Maftir"*. I can see Grandfather in the pauses between the Torah portions peeking into the punctuated volume of the Pentetuch the Gabbai* is holding. He wants to review the cantillation marks of the next passages so he will not make a mistake in reading the text from the Torah scroll. When he reads the Torah, it usually is in a subdued voice heard only in his corner, but I can still hear his clear and distinct voice raised with a flourish for a word marked with a "Pazer"* or "Shalshelet"*.

I recall him, also, sitting on the floor near his wide bed at midnight to recite "Tikkun Hatzoth"*. The whole room is steeped in darkness except for the lone candle in his hand, and his shadow on the wall sways to the rhythm of the lament. His usually firm voice wavers when it is choked by tears: "Remember O Lord what has happened to us . . ." I look at him at that moment and my heart overflows with endless love for him. I turn over in my bed, which is his bed, too, and fall back into a sweet sleep.

I remember the Friday afternoon in the public bath. Grandfather lies always on the highest shelf, where the steam is densest, for he loved the thick, choking steam. He whips himself with a little broom of willow twigs, and from time to time he dunks his head in a pail of cool water and grabs a bit of conversation with his neighbor, Reb Mendl. Wet from head to toe, he finally descends to the floor to urge me to ascend to the upper reaches, to benefit from the recuperative powers of the thick vapor. But I am afraid of the choking steam and beg to be excused. He finally relents and compromises by taking me up to the middle shelf. I surrender my body to the sturdy arms of the old man and indulge in the pleasure of the relaxing, steamy heat, which seems to penetrate every part of my body. Afterwards we go down to submerge in the "Mikva"* in a euphoric mood, chuckling merrily.

Grandfather's outstanding trait was a boundless love for God and man. Every morning, at dawn, he submerged his body in the Mikva and from there proceeded to the first "Minyan"* for early morning worship. Then he would review a lesson in one of the tractates of the Talmud before he returned home for breakfast. Breakfast was an opportunity to recite a few chapters of the Book of Psalms, since not a minute of his time must be wasted. He then asked leave of Grandmother to go out again to discharge some public duties: A sick man needs nursing care; there is a woman in labor to whom the Polish doctor Tschekovsky must be brought in a hurry; he is needed to sit at the bedside of a dying man during the last hours; a funeral — participation in which is reckoned as an ultimate act of kindness; a circumcision — an event which exempts him from reciting the "Tahnun" (prayers of supplication); finding a free meal for transients who had not been invited for lunch by any of the worshippers in the synagogue at the second "Minyan"; a meeting with the emissary from one of the charitable institutions of Jerusalem, who was looking for a notable of the town to accompany him on his rounds of the homes of the rich; visiting a group of Hasidim who were observing the anniversary of the death of their "Rebbe" with much singing and drinking. He might be diverted from his routine by a poor Jew standing outside his house looking for a "tenth man" to complete the "Minyan" in his house on the occasion of Shiva (the seven days of mourning following the death of a close relative). Once he was enlisted by old Reb Kalman, the innkeeper, to help him drag a drunken peasant to a corner where the unconscious man could sleep it off. In short, day in day out, a Jew is a "messenger of mercy" to all in need, and he must fulfill the commandment of "thou shalt surely assit him". The needs of the community are manifold; time is short and the work of charity is long; the workers are few and God forbid that a Jew like Grandfather should be lazy. Grandmother in the store will forgive him if he is a bit late. She surely knows that her husband is not wasting his time.

There is no doubt that on a day when business is not heavy it is permissible to tarry in the fulfillment of charitable command- ments. He is filled with compassion for suffering humanity and is ready to do good deeds — the seemingly insignificant as well as the obviously urgent and important. By virtue of his initiative the needy will be helped and the contributors will not be the losers. For what is man if not a servant of the Lord with all his heart and might and a true brother to his fellowmen, who are always yearning for love which is not dependent upon ulterior motives? That is why he leaves the house at dawn and returns at mid-morning, after giving the Lord a little help with His work.

When he enters the store, if Grandmother seems cross, he tries to placate her with a few witty remarks. If, on the other hand, she is in a good mood, he turns at once to his chores in the store and in the house. In the store he is his wife's assistant: keeping the records straight, making out the customer's bills, wrapping the purchased articles neatly and securely, making light conversation with the steady clients among the peasantry, and above all, carrying out the instruction of the "manager" — Grandmother.

I have an indelible recollection of the friendly and polite banter Grandfather and Grandmother maintained with Panie (Mrs.) Krasnesielsky and with the venerable Anton over glasses of tea. These two were our best customers and often frequented the store on days when there was little business.

Grandfather: Good morning, Mrs. Krasnesielsky!

Mrs. Krasnesielsky: Good morning, Paine Moshke!

Grandfather: I see that you are still quite lively — eh?

Mrs. K: Praise the Lord, quite well; and you Moshke?

Grandfather: Baruch Ha-Shem (blessed be the Lord)! One must not be sinful — we eat and drink and bless His ineffable Name.

Mrs. K: May you be blessed, Paine Moshke. You are a God-fearing man.

Grandfather: May God bless you and your whole family.

The good woman would often bring us a small pitcher of sweet cream or a big bottle of sour milk and hand it to Grandmother with the blessing: "Enjoy it in good health". Grandmother in turn, would take out a cake or some biscuits and hand them to the woman with tender affection.

Venerable Anton has poor vision and deficient hearing. Every time he comes he is served a glass of tea fortified with Vishniak (cherry brandy). It disappears in a few gulps, and when another is proffered, he beams with gratitude and says: "If only all the Jews were like you Moshke! You have a true Christian heart!" Grandfather inquires after his health, bending down to shout in his deaf ear, and wishes him long life and good health. Anton thanks him and begins to complain about the dishonest cattle merchants in town. They buy from him at the lowest prices yet are delinquent in making payments on time. Grandfather waits until he finishes pouring out his wrath, then hands him another glass of tea laced with brandy. The old man relaxes and asks: "Well Moshke, what is your wish now? Which of your Jews needs an extention of his payment on the debt that he owes me?" Grandfather describes the predicament of the debtor — his sick wife, his crumbling house, but before he can finish Anton says,

"Do not waste your breath, I will do as you say. But see to it that the good-for-nothing pays up the capital; as for the interest, you reckon the amount accrued, and you may deduct half of it as a contribution to your favorite charity. Now go back to your sacred books and don't forget to pray for me."

On days when there was no fair in town, Grandfather used to sit at the table and study a chapter of a Talmud tractate. His voice chanted the inquiry and response quietly and in a monotone. He would study for quite a while before Grandmother served him lunch. He washed his hands, said the blessing before eating, then ate everything that was served to him with great appetite. With the drops of water from the fingerbowl still dripping from his hands, his eyes would seek those of Grandmother, and when their glances met with love and joy in each other, he began to say the Grace after meals. His Grace meant: Thanks to God, just because He is God; to man, because he is only man; and to Grandmother because she is the best of women. Little by little his voice lowered, and when he reached the last verse, "May the Lord give strength to his people, may the Lord bless His people with peace", he leaned his head on his elbow and took a nap after the long hours of toil and drudgery.

In the afternoons, when there were few, if any, customers he did house chores. In the wintertime he chopped wood and cleaned the cellar for the spring and summer. In the evenings he patched old clothes for poor people. After Passover, in the spring, he fixed the roof shingles. In early fall he fetched tree branches and flowers and stored them in the back of the house for the Succah (a booth for the Feast of Tabernackles). In the summer he painted the walls of the house and store. If the work did not require concentration, he recited by heart chapters from the Psalms, the melodious chant reverberating to the far reaches of the house. But when the work required close attention, all we heard were snatches of Hasidic tunes, interspersed with single words and syllables. Toward evening, just before the afternoon-evening worship session, he played with his grandchildren. He picked up my giggling little brother and waved the frightened little boy in the air or gave him a ride on his back. All the while Grandfather shouted with joy and laughter, and made wild and unintelligible sounds — all of which spelled out his conviction that he was the happiest and most fortunate of men.

On the eve of the Sabbath he was irritable and moody, especially in the wintertime when the days are short, the sun sets early and preparations for the Sabbath are numerous. He would easily get upset when we were dilly-dallying, and scolded us with the admonition that the Sabbath would soon be here and we must hurry to complete our chores. But when he returned from the public baths, shiny and well-scrubbed, dressed in his white shirt, silk kaftan and Sabbath hat, he was his usual self again. I accompanied him to the Sabbath service. He would take my hand in his, kiss the Mezuzah* and we would walk with brisk steps to the synagogue. I felt then that he was at peace with the world and with himself, completely under the magic spell of the "Neshama Yetera" ("Supersoul") of the Holy Sabbath.

This mood of mystical exaltation lasted until late Saturday night. His erect stance and beaming face, his curled sideburns and neatly combed beard, his measured speech and slow movements all were redolent of the spiritual splendor of the Sabbath. The Sabbath hymns (during mealtimes on Friday evening and Saturday noon) were sung vigorously, almost triumphantly, except for those chanted at the "Seudah Shelishit"* on Sabbath afternoon, which were rendered in a minor key, softly and sadly, like a lover taking leave of his beloved. Then the still prevalent joy of the Sabbath was tainted with sorrow at its impending departure. When his Hasidic friends from the fellowship of Reb Dovidl of Skvira, were his table guests — all of them well versed in the Rebbe's repertoire of melodies — Grandfather let himself go completely. He led the group in filling the gathering gloom of the dusk hours with songs of glory and adoration to the Almighty, accentuated by the rhythmic tapping and pounding of silverware against the ringing glasses — eyes closed, hearts astir with emotion bodies swaying, the wordless tune emanating from the innermost soul, rising heavenward to the Throne of Glory, as it were.

When I was nine years old, and I had learned by heart ten full pages of the Talmudic tractate "Baba Kama", Grandfather began to prod my mother to let me accompany him on one of his visits to the Rebbe's court in Skvira. At first my mother refused, but she finally gave in to his entreaties. The trip took a whole day. Grandfather kept asking me whether I knew the subject thoroughly, for I was to be tested by none other than the Rebbe himself. On Saturday night he led me to the Rebbe's seat of honor and meekly suggested that his grandson wished to be examined by the Rebbe, while I stood bashfully and tremulously behind him, weak-kneed with apprehension. Reb Dovidl inquired as to the particular subject that I was studying at the time, and when I began to recite with lowered head, I felt Grandfather's reassuring hand holding mine for moral support. The Rebbe followed my little lecture with a few questions, which I answered properly, taking a look from time to time at Grandfather for reassurance. All the while his face shone and tears of joy ran down his cheeks. "My son", the Rebbe concluded the interview, pinching my cheek, "continue studying with zeal, and may your parents rejoice with you". After this adventure Grandfather bought me a little mouth organ as a gift, and my love for him became stronger than ever.

When I was eleven years old, and my teacher for secular subject matter opened up a new wide world of knowledge for me, my Grandfather's attitude toward me changed. When he saw me reading a non-Jewish book, he would taunt me with scornful and derisive expletives, such as: "Treif-Possul" (forbidden), "Hokhmat Yavan" (i.e., philosophy, literally, "Greek Wisdom"), and "Goyishkeit" (gentile life-style). Occasionally he would ask me whether I had taken my lesson with Reb Nathan the Talmud teacher, if I had participated in the afternoon public worship or if I reviewed the biblical portion of the week according to the prescribed method: twice in the original Hebrew and once in the Aramaic translation. These harsh-voiced queries were directed not at me but at my father, who had brought on this "evil". My father had worked hard, and by dint of gruelling study had managed to pass the examination and acquire a matura* certificate. He had also studied law in a university outside Russia. He had, so to speak, taken a look at the enlightened, outside world and been affected by it to the point of demanding that his sons be given a good general education, in addition to their Hebrew studies. For hours on end he discussed the matter with Grandfather and he finally won the argument. From then on Grandfather stopped inviting me to accompany him to a "Kiddush" (refreshments served after public worship on the occasion of a family celebration), or to console mourners. We no longer took our walks in the woods and fields, when he would tell me stories and legends from the Talmud, and top them off in a "song match" of excerpts of the High Holiday liturgy, such as: "Like a shepherd mustering his flock" and "May our song rise in the morning", songs which I had learned in Reb Jacob the Cantor's choir; and our visits to the homes of our friends among the peasants and the townspeople ceased.

About two months before the outbreak of World War I, when I was nearly twelve years old, I passed the competitive examinations for admission to the Geffen Gymnasium in Odessa and started in the 4th grade. When I returned home on vacation dressed in my student's uniform, Grandfather met me at the door and with a surprised look at my outfit, remarked ironically: "The 'goy' (non-Jew) has come home to spend his 'goyish' feast day ..." Neverthless, he embraced me warmly, and when we came into his room and the hour of the afternoon worship was at hand, he urged me to go with him to the synagogue. "Do you still remember the prayers?" he asked, and without waiting for an answer tied a sash around my waist (a Hasisdic custom, to divide the "profane" lower part of the body from the upper, "sacred" part) and commanded me to lead the congregation in prayer. In chanting the text of the service I made sure to employ all the cantorial flourishes. In the intermission between the afternoon and evening services he put his hand upon my shoulder as a sign of appreciation and said: "Good, very good — you will surely be a good Jew, in spite of everything".

When the war broke out I did not return to Odessa. Grandfather, even though he did not say it openly, was glad that my secular studies had ceased. His attitude toward me changed for the better, and, again, we became greatly attached to each other.

The war left its mark upon the town. The number of deserters from the front increased daily, and there was no home without a "hare", as we nicknamed them. Raids and searches by the military police were daily occurrences, and when a few deserters were caught there was much "wailing and gnashing of teeth". Little by little the chances of making a living diminished, with artisans and petty tradesmen being especially affected. Grandfather and his welfare-worker companions — Jacob the Cantor, Abraham-Joshua the ritual slaughter, Isaac Kanevsky and Hannah-Rivah the Pot

Peddler — were very busy. They worked to feed the hungry, to clothe the ragged and to heal the sick. At that time one of the richest men in town, Reb Yudl Moreinis, died. It happened to be Thursday, and the members of the Burial Society decided to collect a "contribution" of a thousand rubles from the family of the deceased, in addition to the normal costs of the funeral, and to use the money for charity. Should the members of the family refuse to pay up, they would delay the funeral indefinitely, which was a grave sin and an insult to the deceased and his family. There was great dissension in the Society and much contention in the town at large over this unprecedented act. Some maintained that the law be set aside and the opportunity to "collect the debt" not be lost. Others insisted that such high-handed methods were akin to blackmail, and that the purification of the body and the sewing of the shrouds be done at once, so as not to delay the funeral until after the Sabbath.

Grandfather ran from place to place: from the home of the deceased to the quarters of the Burial Society; from the house of the Rabbi to the house of Mr. Markev, the richest man in town and one of the late Reb Yudl's closest friends. Late that night a meeting was called. I went with Grandfather to see the heirs several times in succession and then to the synagogue to report to the anxious townspeople about the results of the latest negotiations and the expected financial settlement. I carried the lantern to light the way in the dark streets. I heard Grandfather argue with the heirs about the duty of lending support to their less fortunate fellow men. His argument was fortified by learned quotations, such as: "The needs of Thy People are numerous" and "Thou shalt surely assist him". But the more he piled reason upon reason for their obligation to meet the demands of the burial society leaders, the greater grew their obstinate refusal to comply. Finally, Grandfather's patience gave way. He picked up the heavy cane he carried for support and handed it to the eldest son of the deceased. In a tone of command he said to him: "Take this cane and beat me with it. I cannot come to the meeting with empty hands!" He burst into tears and held on with trembling hands to the table which stood in the middle of the room. Finally, he slid to the floor in a gesture of mourning for the living in the house of the dead. I sat down next to him on the floor and wiped his face, which was wet with tears. When the heirs saw the dignified old man so humiliated and shaken by their greedy obstinacy, they held a little conference, and the eldest, who held Grandfather's cane, raised him up, returned the cane and announced: "We shall do as you say, Reb Moishe; please go and tell them to hasten with the preparations for the funeral". And that very night the townspeople took part in the burial service for the venerable Reb Yudl. Grandfather was one of the pallbearers and would not allow Gedalia, Reb Yudl's nephew and Squire Antoshka's steward, to take his place, as is customary on such occasion, but bravely and vigorously, he carried his burden to the cemetery gates.

I recall still another incident. It happened on a miserable autumn day, when the mud was deep and a cold northern wind blew incessantly. Suddenly, ear-splitting cries were heard in the distance. Grandfather put on his coat and hurried to the saloon of Reb Mottl Altman, from where the cries and sighs originated. In spite of his order to stay home, I ran after him. When we got there we saw a circle of men, Jews and Gentiles, surrounding Ivan Kapusta and his three sons, who were wrestling each other on the muddy ground. Ivan, a tall sturdy peasant who was famous in the whole province for his courage and prowess, was giving his sons a severe beating and kicking their faces into a bloody pulp with his hobnailed boots. It was amazing with what agility he managed to rise every time the three sons tackled his legs to good purpose. He attacked the younger men like a predatory animal, biting one's ear, choking the other, and giving the third a swift kick in the groin.

The members of Reb Mottl's household had raised the alarm and each seemed to outdo the other with his bellowing "Gevald" (help!). Grandfather pushed himself through the circle of on-lookers, approached close to the writhing gladiators, and in a loud voice shouted: "S t o p!" Ivan turned his head toward Grandfather and warned him: "Panie Moshke, don't mix into a matter that doesn't concern you! Get away from here or I'll beat you within an inch of your life." But Grandfather raised his cane and scolded him: "Ivan, you are known as a lover of people who performs acts of kindness to his fellowmen. Control your temper and forgive your sons! Must I, your close friend, lower the cane upon your head?" The onlookers held their breath and a sudden stillness reigned. Ivan embraced Grandfather and planted a kiss upon his cheek. Immediately, the sons rose and returned to the saloon, from where they soon emerged with a bottle of whiskey, two lit candles, a loaf of bread and a shaker of salt on a tray. They came close to their father in abject humility and pleaded: "Please, Batiushka (little father), forgive your sinful sons, and may God be with you."

Ivan was astounded at this dramatic transformation in the attitude of his sons. He shook Grandfather's hand vigorously and hugged his sons. The innkeeper held the tray and the onlookers applauded the sudden disappearance of the enmity. Reb Mottl invited everybody inside and treated them to expensive drinks. When we left the saloon Grandfather put his hand on my shoulder and said: "Come, let us go to the synagogue for afternoon services, and let us thank God for His great mercy, for I do not deserve the mercies which He has bestowed upon me this day."

That year on the Fifteenth of Shevat (Arbor Day, also known as the New Year of the Trees in Israel), my grandmother died. Our house was full of people, among them my father who had been hastily recalled from the town of Geissin, where he worked in an armament plant. Father walked about like a shadow, not able to find a place to sit down, while Grandfather stood leaning on the bookcase looking into the distance dazed and shocked. It was night, but the full moon seemed to lack its usual luster as it shone upon the funeral procession. In the court of the synagogue, Reb Jacob the Cantor chanted the burial prayer. His chanting was steeped in sorrow, and filled with sadness were the hearts of all who accompanied the deceased to her last resting place. Grandfather whispered in my ear: "You will not go to the cemetery; go to your uncle's house and wait there for me." The women and children returned to their homes, and Aunt Bracha, the wife of my uncle, "little" Moishe, brought me a pitcher of water to wash my hands to cleanse them from the impurities of the dead. Then I entered the room and sat at the edge of the bed waiting for Grandfather to return. My aunt fell asleep but I was frightened and puzzled by how strange my Grandfather had looked. The light of the kerosene lamp went out. A mood of deep depression gripped me and the shadows on the wall frightened me. Just then Grandfather entered, knelt at the edge of the bed, took my head in his arms and said: "Weep, my child, weep, and you will feel better." Embracing each other we wept quietly, so as not to awaken the living in the house, and so that the sound of our weeping should not reach Grandmother in her last resting place.

Time went on but life was bereft of joy. Grandfather was always morose — his humming was sad and his sighing frequent and heavy. Our talks about the strategies of the Russian and German armies were most discouraging, and our hearts prophesied evil events in the future.

When the news reached us of the oppressions, robberies and killings, and the leaders of the community sought ways and means of meeting the impending peril, Grandfather became more energetic. Gone were the sighs, and the shadow disappeared from his face. His main preoccupation was supervision over the building of shelters in the basements, in the attics, and behind the tile ovens. And although all who built such refuges kept their location a secret, they were happy to trust Grandfather and to receive his advice and assistance. At first only expensive merchandise, good clothing, gold and silver vessels, were hidden away. But in time as news of pogroms in neighboring towns reached us, the shelters were made "habitable" for their owners. In our house Grandfather dug a deep hole in a wall leading to the alley, and after a great deal of work widened it into a shelter which was 10 feet wide and 8 feet long. The entrance to the shelter was covered with plaster and whitewashed to look like the rest of the wall. And it was filled with all kinds of objects so that no hollow sound should be heard when the robbers would bang against it with their rifle butts in their search for hidden valuables. Though some of these hiding places became the graves of those who sought shelter there, in a number of cases they served their purpose and saved many lives.

The tenth of Tammuz (July 18th) in the year 1919 was a scorching summer day. Early in the morning the news spread that the forces of the Ukrainian chieftain Tutuniuk were nearing our settlement. Quickly the town square, where groups of people had been standing discussing the frequent battles between the units of the Red Army and the forces of the Ukrainian nationalist leader Petlura, was emptied. Not a living soul was in sight. Everyone locked himself in behind heavy doors and bolts and hid in secret shelters. The terror of death descended on the community. An eerie silence reigned, replete with mortal fear. It was like the ominous silence before a storm.

We, the children, were ordered to hide in the attic. Father left the house to attend the meeting of the rescue committee. On his way he was surrounded by a group of Gaidamacks, who took him to the headquarters of the chief to be kept as a hostage. When Grandfather stepped outside, he saw his son being led away. Grandfather ran to the house of the priest to seek his aid. The air was already filled with sounds of terror and weeping and the smashing of doors and window panes. The pogrom had begun. When Grandfather heard from the priest that the chieftain of the band demanded a "contribution" of money, and promised to free the hostages, including his son, when the money was delivered, he ran quickly to the homes of the wealthy men in town; and when he could not find them, he looked for them in the shelters; and if they were not there either, he hastened to the homes of their friends among the peasants. Within an hour or so he had a bag full of paper money, which he took to the priest's house and left in his safekeeping.

Meanwhile, several courageous men emerged from their hiding places and collected sacks of flour, blankets and boots to add to the monetary "contribution" — all in accordance with Tutiuniuk's orders. These, too, were deposited in the house of the priest. When the whole tribute was carried in the wagon of the priest's curate toward the chieftain's headquarters, Grandfather walked behind the wagon. When they arrived, they saw the group of six hostages standing in a row, facing a line of armed soldiers who were waiting for the chieftain's command. Tutiuniuk had the wagon emptied. This done, he gave the order to shoot.

Toward evening our mother came to see us. She embraced us lovingly, but we felt that a terrible misfortune had befallen us. Without saying a word she motioned to us to follow her. We hurried to the synagogue where a great crowd milled around in the vestibule. I heard that the partisans had left the town and that a party of volunteers had gone to the arena of the slaughter to bring back the bodies of the martyrs. Isaac K. took my hand and led me into the main hall of the synagogue. Inside, I saw on the floor, to the west of the central pulpit facing the entrance, a body covered by a white sheet. At its head two tapers were burning. Isaac K.

pressed my hand tightly and in a trembling voice and broken sentences explained: "This martyr we brought into the sanctuary itself . . . The head of the community . . . He sacrificed his life . . . An irreversible loss . . . Woe unto us — and He who dwells in the heaven is silent. . ." With trembling knees I approached the body.

My Grandfather was standing at the feet staring into space, as if he were seeking an answer to the riddle of Jewish life and to the mystery of his only son's death. And Reb Isaac was walking to and fro, clasping his hands and wailing. The cries from the vestibule reached me; the sound of loud weeping was growing — the people had come to the synagogue to take leave of their martyred leader forever. . .

The funeral procession started. Thirty-five bodies were gathered and placed into one wagon. Several young men stood around it as an honor guard. The order was given to proceed to the cemetery, but many women held on to the wheels of the wagon, as if to stop it from rolling. From the synagogue they carried father out on a board; they raised him onto their shoulders. Jacob, the cantor, went in front reciting prayers. Evening shadows descended on the town. People began to whisper that the dark would bring the danger of an ambush. The crowd dispersed.

At the cemetery there was much work to be done. Sons and fathers dug the huge common grave. In the light of the moon the work lasted until midnight. From time to time the stillness was shattered by shots which struck fear into every heart and apprehension for loved ones left alone at home. Before the work was finished two peasant women brought loaves of bread and pitchers of water. Those who felt faint from hunger ate and drank at the open grave. Their strength was giving out and there was still much to do. Finally, when the grave was dug, thirty six boards bearing the bodies of the martyrs were lowered into it.

Two days after the funeral, my sister who was brought home from the city of Uman, came down with typhus. She thrashed about on her bed in high fever. Grandfather nursed her and would not let anyone else touch the girl. A week passed and things quieted down, even though the town was still steeped in deep mourning. A rumor spread that a troop of Ukrainian cavalrymen was approaching the town. Granfather immediately asked for sheets and ice-water, wrapped the sick girl in the iced sheets and hid her in the shelter. He stood guard at the wall, his eyes riveted to the door waiting for the bandits to appear any moment and ready to do battle with them. Three of them came into the house, demanding: "Where are the women?" Grandfather told them that there were no women in the house. One of them approached him and hit him in the face, pulled his sabre from its scabbard and shouted: "Cursed Jew, if you won't show me at once the place where you hid the women I'll cut off your ear!" But Grandfather insisted that there were no hiding places and no women in the house. Then the second soldier took out his knife and cut off my Grandfather's earlobe, while the third one kicked him to the ground. When they left, my mother, who had been in hiding, hastened to bandage the wound. Grandfather stood up, took a bottle of alcohol out of the table drawer, and signaled an order to close the outside door, which led to the marketplace. Then he opened the shelter, carefully pulled out the patient wrapped in the cool blanket, hoisted her on his shoulders, and left the house ordering us not to follow him. When he returned, he informed us that she was safe in the house of old Anton, and that after he had rubbed her body with the alcohol, her fever had subsided.

Before many days had passed I reached my sixteenth birthday, and made ready to leave the country for Palestine by crossing the Bessarabian border. My mother sewed for me a linen waistcoat with a hidden pocket in which to secret a few bills of paper money. Grandfather hollowed out the heel of my right shoe as a cache for some gold coins. At dawn, when the coach came to fetch me, Grandfather handed me a "Talith Katan"*, whose fringes he had examined the previous night, and a little sack with phylacteries, whose absolutely perfect script was attested to by the scribe who had made them. I took off my jacket and Grandfather put the "Talith Katan" over my head. Then he placed the sack with the phylacteries among my personal effects. He then took me to the "Mezuzah"*, raised himself and kissed it with his mouth, then waited for me to kiss it with my fingers. "Take leave of your family", he said quietly. After my tearful farewell to my mother, sister and younger brother, Grandfather went with me into the street. The coach was surrounded by many men, women and children who came to see us off. Grandfather embraced me, kissed me on the forehead, and in a voice steeped in sorrow, declared:

"Remember, my son, that we are sending you into the unknown alien lands. Keep in mind your place of origin. I do not know if I will ever see you again, but until my last day my thoughts will be with you wherever you may be. . . ." The coach began to move, and I was weeping inwardly: "Will I see my Grandfather again?"

I have not had the privilege.

Glossary

Alyiah — Hebrew for the ascent or "the going up" to Palestine or Israel. The abstract noun ALYIAH means immigration or re-migration to the Land of Israel.

Auto-Emancipation — The title of a pamphlet in which the author (Dr. Leon Pinsker, 1821-1891) advocated emigration, and acquirement of land (preferable in Palestine) as the road to self-emancipation of Jews.

Bialik, H.N. — Famous Hebrew poet and scholar, considered the Jewish National poet (1872-1934).

Bund — Jewish Socialist party in Eastern Europe, organized in Wilna in 1897, as a union of the Russian Jewish Socialist groups. The Bund maintained an attitude of antagonism to Zionism, but supported the rights of national-cultural minorities.

Ein-Yaakov — A popular anthology of Midrashic tales and commentaries.

Gabbai — Synagogue leader, usually honored with the right to stand at the side of the Torah reader, to prompt him if he should make a mistake in reading from the unpunctuated and unvocalized text.

Good Shabbes — Yiddish greetings for the Sabbath.

Good Yomtev — Yiddish greeting for the festivals.

Gaidamaks — Ukrainian bands of Cossacks.

Gimatriot — Substitution of one Hebrew word for another, whose letters when considered as numbers add up to the same number of letters of the other word. For example, the Hebrew lettering of the word Yayin (Hebrew for wine) constitutes the numbers 10 plus 10 plus 50, equals 70; the word Sod (Hebrew for secret) numbers 60 plus 6 plus 4, equals 70; thus in Gimatriot the sum of one word is equal to the sum of the other.

Gymnasia — The European High School.

Hagomel — A benediction which expresses to God gratitude for surviving calamity.

Hakafot — The circuit-like procession with the Torah scrolls on Simhat Torah the day following the Succot festival.

HaShiloah — A Hebrew monthly published in Odessa at the turn of the century.

Hashomer — Literally, the Guard, organized in 1908. The self-defense organization in Palestine, consisting of agricultural workers who defended Jewish settlements against Arab -attacks.

HaTzefirah — Hebrew daily newspaper published in Warsaw.

Havdalah — Literally, separation, the blessings recited over a cup of wine, marking the end of the Sabbath.

HeHalutz — Literally, the pioneer, a Zionist youth organization which stressed individual fulfillment through work and life as farmers in a commune in Palestine.

Heid-Hazman — Hebrew daily newspaper.

ICA — Initials for The Jewish Colonization Association, founded by Baron de Hirsch in 1891 to assist and promote the migration of Jews from Europe and to establish colonies in the newly adopted countries.

Kartofel — Yiddish for potato.

Kaddish — The mourner's prayer in Hebrew and Aramaic.

Kibbutz — A collective farm settlement in Palestine — Israel. A labor commune in which all members bear relation to each other as members of a family.

Knishes — Yiddish word for a delicacy made from dough filled with grain or chopped meat and baked.

Kreplakh — Rolled dough filled with either cheese or meat and boiled in water.

Kugel — Yiddish for a noodle pudding served on Sabbaths and festivals.

Maftir — The last phrases of the weekly portion of the Pentateuch read on Sabbaths and festivals. The person called to Maftir generally reads the "Haftarah", or the prophetic selection for the day.

Maskil — The Hebrew term for an enlighted person who synthesizes secular and Judaic cultures.

Mezuzah — A metal or wooden case in which the passages from Deuteronomy 6:4-10; 11: 13-22 are inscribed on parchment, attached to the doorpost of the house.

Menorah — Candlestick.

Mikvah — Ritual bath for the purification of the body as ordained in Leviticus 11:36. The bath is deep enough for complete immersion of the body.

Minyian — A quorum of ten Jews to engage in public worship.

Pale of Settlement — A Russian territory of 14 provinces accessible to the Jews for permanent residence.

Pazer — A musical note for a word in Scriptures, which calls for special intonation.

Petah Tikvah — An agricultural settlement in Palestine established in 1878.

Purim — The festival observed annually on the 14th day of the month of Adar, to commemorate the deliverance of the Jews in Persia, as related in the biblical book of Esther. It is a festival, the religious observance of which narrowed to the reading of the Scroll, Megillat Esther, at the regular services. It calls for no abstinence from work. Its games, merrymaking, sending of gifts, masquerades are an expression of fun and jest.

Second Alyiah — Groups of young men and women, imbued with the spirit of Socialist Zionism, who settled in Palestine during the first decade of the 20th century.

Seudah-Shlishit — The meal after Minhah, the late afternoon Sabbath service.

Shelishi — Literally, "third", the third portion of the weekly reading of the Penteuch on Sabbaths.

Shalshelet — Same as Pazer chanted with greater emphasis.

Shloshim — Literally "thirty", the month of bereavement.

Shiveah — The seven days of mourning after burial.

Simhat Torah — "Rejoicing over the Law", celebrated on the 23rd day of the month of Tishri. The ritual of the festival is well described in its name, and its motive is the preservation of the continuity of the Reading of the Law. So, when the last lines of Deutcronomy have been recited, the end of the Penteteuch is immediately followed by the reading of the opening chapter of Genesis. The Scrolls of the Law are carried in procession, followed by children waiving flags at both the evening and morning services. This joyous ritual is elaborated by dancing.

Shma Yisrael — "Hear O Israel, The Lord Our God, The Lord Is One" (Deut. 6:4). These are the words of the confession of faith.

Succot (sing. Succah) — The Feast of Tabernacles, celebrated for seven days beginning with the 15th of Tishri.

Talit Katan — A small prayer shawl worn under the upper garments.

Tahanun — Penitential type of prayer recited on week days.

Tchernichowsky's poem — "This Will be Our Revenge" was translated from the Hebrew by Dr. Shalom Spiegel.

Tikun Hatzot — Excerpts from biblical texts and from liturgical poems of lamentations bewailing the destruction of Jerusalem and the exile from the Holy Land.

Viduy — The Hebrew term denoting the prayer before death.

Zemirot — Liturgical chants for Sabbath and festivals.